Mary's Way

"In *Mary's Way*, you'll discover Judy Klein's powerful story. If you're not careful, you'll find yourself staying up late to read it, getting invested in the lessons she shares, and adjusting your viewpoint on many things. Klein is a companion who every mom will want on their own journey."

Sarah Reinhard
Catholic writer, blogger, and editor of *Word By Word*

"In *Mary's Way*, Judy Landrieu Klein takes us on her spiritual journey through her adult years as wife and mother. Her stories invite us into a deeper relationship with the Lord and the Blessed Mother, encouraging us to 'yield to God and say yes to him in whatever life brings.' Klein's 'yes' to God, modeled after the Blessed Virgin Mary's fiat, can be our 'yes,' too."

Maria Morera Johnson
Author of *My Badass Book of Saints*

"Through vivid personal stories of suffering and joy, Klein shares her own mother's heart and how she came to know the most blessed of all mothers, Mary. *Mary's Way* is about both—the power of our own maternal prayers and Mary's motherly interceding for us."

Pat Gohn
Author of *Blessed, Beautiful, and Bodacious*

"With poignant and relatable storytelling, Klein invites us into the intimacy of her profound sorrows as a wife, mother, sister, and daughter in the hopes that the lessons of faith she learned will benefit us in our own struggles. If you're a mother or grandmother, you need *Mary's Way*."

Kitty Cleveland
Catholic author, speaker, and musician

Mary's Way

The Power of Entrusting Your Child to God

JUDY LANDRIEU KLEIN

AVE MARIA PRESS AVE Notre Dame, Indiana

© 2016 by Judy Landrieu Klein

Foreword © 2016 by Lisa M. Hendey

All rights reserved. No part of this book may be used or reproduced in any manner whatsoever, except in the case of reprints in the context of reviews, without written permission from Ave Maria Press©, Inc., P.O. Box 428, Notre Dame, IN 46556, 1-800-282-1865.

Founded in 1865, Ave Maria Press is a ministry of the United States Province of Holy Cross.

www.avemariapress.com

Paperback: ISBN-13 978-1-59471-669-0

E-book: ISBN-13 978-1-59471-670-6

Cover image "Madonna and Child" © Tracy Christianson, PortraitsofSaints.com.

Cover and text design by Katherine Robinson.

Printed and bound in the United States of America.

Library of Congress Cataloging-in-Publication Data is available.

To my heavenly

Mother Mary

and my earthly mother Phyllis—

with great love and gratitude.

CONTENTS

Chapter 7
THE RESURRECTION: HOW GOD MAKES THINGS NEW

FOREWORD

As I travel around the country praying and serving in the company of mothers and grandmothers, I have noted some consistent themes that arise regardless of the size, economic profile, or cultural backdrop of the parish or organization hosting me. I believe I've noticed their omnipresence because they are struggles I often face in my own life as a wife and mother.

How do I know that I'm doing enough to serve my family?

What can I do to better share my love for my faith with my children?

How will I ensure they won't drift away from the Church when they leave our home?

When will I ever feel like I have enough time for daily prayer?

At this point, I know my own spiritual journey and shortcomings well enough to avoid trying to give simple answers to these profoundly challenging questions. My most common response these days is to assure my new sisters in Christ that they will be in my prayers. But, I always ask for their prayers for me and for my family as well.

And I'm serious when I make these humble requests for prayer. Because the more diligently I trod my vocational path as a Catholic mom, the more cognizant I am of life's trials. Without prayer as a lifeblood, I am lost. Yet, when I feel most thoroughly overwhelmed, I typically have to admit that in my desire to be all things to all people, I have given short shrift to my Creator. I know in my heart that time spent in prayer for those I love most is the very best way that I can serve them. But all too often in this selfie-centric, Pinterest-perfect world of ours, my priorities fall out of order.

St. Elizabeth Ann Seton, one of my favorite spiritual intercessors, was herself a wife and mother before founding the Sisters of Charity religious order in her widowhood. A convert to the faith, Mother Seton—the first American-born saint to be canonized—knew more than her fair share of trials. Yet it was through her moments of greatest torment and challenge that she found her true faith in Christ.

Years ago, I copied some of St. Elizabeth Ann's words on prayer in one of my spiritual journals. That quotation, transcribed in a raw moment of motherly self-doubt, has become a reminder for me of the timelessness of motherhood and its priorities: "We must pray without ceasing, in every occurrence and employment of our lives—that prayer which is rather a habit of lifting up the heart to God as in a constant communication with Him."

I believe this book you and I hold in our hands today will soon become as well loved as my journaled memento of Mother Seton's wisdom. When I first met Judy Klein, I saw her through the prism of my casual friendship with her lovely and talented daughter Kara. Knowing Kara's heart and the deep font of her faith, I mentally credited Judy with having done some pretty amazing mothering. In this matter, I believe I was right.

What I didn't know then, but what I've learned in the last few years in moments of private prayer and conversation with Judy, are the many excruciating challenges this lovely woman has had to face along her life's journey. When you're in Judy's presence, you can't help but be entranced not only by her physical beauty but even more so by the deep well of spiritual wisdom that exudes from her.

But it's only when you sit and listen to Judy's stories that you begin to get a glimmer of the light of Christ in her heart. Judy's is not one of those sticky-sweet holy card testimonials. Rather, Judy's witness draws you closer to Jesus Christ through our Blessed Mother precisely because this is a woman who has confronted some of life's most harrowing challenges. She has faced torment, trials with her children, and even the death of loved ones. Through it all, Judy has grown ever more firm in her faith. When I learned over time the details of Judy's life, I found myself even more profoundly in awe of the way in which this wife and mother "walks the talk."

To say that I'm thrilled beyond measure at the publication of this, the newest book in our CatholicMom.com partnership with Ave Maria Press, is an understatement. Judy has gifted all of us with a modern-day template for praying with and for our beloved children and spouses. By grappling with and ultimately accepting the role of Mary in her own life, she invites us into our own consideration of our Blessed Mother's deeply held desire to be a constant companion for us in our prayer.

I now feel better equipped to respond to those deep and turbulent questions I mentioned earlier . . . the ones that dwell in the hearts of just about every Catholic mom I know. Along with inviting them to pray with and for me, I will be pointing them to the spiritual friendship of Judy Klein and to this book. And I believe by the time you've finished these pages, you will join me in thanking my friend Judy for the very open sharing of not only her tragedies but her quiet triumphs too.

I invite you to share this book with a special friend in your life and to join me in prayer for Judy, for her family, and for every woman who desires to more deeply give God her yes by deeply loving and serving her family. May our Blessed Mother be our advocate, our model, and our trusted companion along life's winding path to heaven.

Lisa M. Hendey

Founder of *CatholicMom.com*

 Saving Motherhood

[Women] will be saved through motherhood,
provided [they] persevere in faith and love and
holiness, with self-control.

~1 Timothy 2:15

One of my great dreams in life was to become a mother. I have vivid memories of playing with both my baby dolls and my baby brothers, lost in the pretend world of motherhood, yearning with everything in me to have my own child. My sister and I practically paid the neighbors to let us babysit, and we were more than happy to clean kitchens, sweep floors, or do any other household chores for the privilege of holding their babies. Even as a child, the smell of a baby left me intoxicated. I was completely obsessed.

I was nothing less than convinced that I would be a wonderful, competent mother. My mother had ten children, and I wanted six. I ended up with three girls and two boys, plus a little soul in heaven. It was not exactly what I expected, but then nothing about motherhood has been. I didn't expect it to be so intensely gratifying. And I certainly didn't expect it to be so challenging.

Our first daughter, Kara, was born two weeks early following a long day of last-minute Christmas shopping. Due to arrive on January 6, she came on Christmas Eve during a bitter winter freeze. I could hardly wait to get her home to settle into our new life together. Eagerly anticipating her arrival, I had practiced a morning ritual for months that included going into her nursery and bringing a tiny outfit to my just-waking husband, Bernie, to "dance" on the bed, trying to picture the little person who would be wearing it soon. It was all going to be smiles and roses.

It took mere days after her birth to figure out that I knew almost nothing about mothering. It had never occurred to me that I might have a baby with severe colic, and Kara's screaming left me at a total loss. Nothing I tried seemed to help. Neither walking the floors for hours at night nor rocking her did a thing to calm her down—nor did the colic drops, the warm water bottle, or the doctor's last-resort suggestion of placing her tummy down on our running dryer, over which I stood sometimes for an hour or more in the middle of the night trying to soothe her little stomach. So much for my confidence in my competence! I quickly learned that if I was going to survive this thing called motherhood, I'd better start to *pray*. Pray I did— and I've been praying nonstop ever since! And like every mother who's ever lived, I've had *plenty* to pray about.

Each phase of motherhood has brought new challenges and surprises, and each stage has taught me how to pray in deeper and more soul-surrendering ways, for both my children and myself. I have learned over nearly thirty years that prayer, like motherhood, is dynamic and can effect change in us and in the world around us. Both of these outcomes are good and necessary as we move forward in the spiritual journey and in the vocation of motherhood.

The life of a praying mother often involves two specific types of prayer: the prayer of petition and the prayer of surrender. In the prayer of petition, we pray *for* our children or ourselves, asking God to intervene in our lives in a particular way. This may be the way we pray most often as mothers. Thankfully, I've seen quite a few miracles happen through petitioning prayer, some of which I will share in this book. Those are the prayer stories that people love to hear because they build our faith and trust in God and in his amazing power.

But what happens when our appeals seemingly go unanswered, or when life unfolds in a way that we consider negative or even disastrous, no matter how hard we pray or how many times we ask God for something? It is in these instances that God invites us to learn the power of prayerful surrender. It's a prayer that can bring real peace, and it often brings us to deeper conversion and inner transformation. It sometimes takes many hard lessons and countless wrestling matches with God to learn to surrender, and it's something we must practice as we go. But surrendering prayer is worth leaning into and learning well because, in the end, learning to yield to God and say yes to him in whatever life brings changes *us*.

May It Be Done to Me According to Your Word (Lk 1:38)

What exactly is the prayer of surrender? It involves the ongoing practice of opening our hands to God and releasing ourselves and others to him in a way that permits grace to move. It includes developing the habit of giving up our attempts to control people and events by intentionally giving them to God. And it encompasses yielding our will to God's providential will through faith, inviting him to empower us to see our lives through his transcendent perspective instead of through the lens of our own limited human understanding. Learning the prayer of surrender is not a one-shot wonder. It takes much practice, perseverance, and patience, plus the example of those who have lived it extraordinarily well.

When considering surrendering prayer, there is no better example to ponder than Mary, the Mother of Jesus. Surely, the Blessed Mother had to surrender her Son to the Father in heaven repeatedly during his life, ultimately giving Jesus up in prayer on the Cross. The unfolding of the Son of God's life presented many formidable challenges for his Mother, and in each trial Mary had to learn to yield to God more fully. Each relinquishment was an act of love, and every surrender became an open space for *more* love. Therein lies the mystery of the prayer of surrender—a mystery we can learn at the feet of Mary.

The power of a mother's prayer consists in offering her child and herself to God in a way that makes *more* space for his love—a challenge that's easier said than done! It is a challenge we will consider at length in this book, using scenes from Mary's life as our guide. We will follow the Blessed Mother from the annunciation to the Resurrection, seeing in each moment of her life with Christ what we can prayerfully glean from her example. We will learn how she submitted herself and her Son to the Father unceasingly and how her surrender made space for the expansion of God's infinite love in this all-too-imperfect world.

When I first became a wife and mother, I was pretty convinced that I could exert my will on my husband, my children, and the world around me and make them line up with my expectations. Truth be told, I was somewhat of a control freak, and I expected life to fall in line with my plans. When things didn't go my way, I became extremely angry, and I even got angry with God. Thankfully, life had a way of consistently teaching me two extremely important lessons: there is a God and it ain't me, and I am not in control. Does this ring a bell for you?

I look back with some fascination on my control-freak days because it's clear to me now that my stance concerning my life directly reflected my stance with God, which was, I love you, but my life will be according to *my* will. Such a stance is not uncommon in women, and it can manifest itself in any number of ways, evidenced through our attitudinal disposition toward God and those in our lives. We can attempt to exert our will on the world around us, wanting reality to line up with our wishes, and then find ourselves frustrated and angry when that doesn't happen. We are tempted to manipulate, dominate, or control so that things go our way, rejecting the Marian stance of active abandonment to God in favor of Eve's posture of grasping to get what she wanted. We've struggled with the same darn problem ever since the Fall, beginning with Eve and continuing through the generations, and it can even show up in the way we pray. So much of our prayer life can be spent telling God what to do and how he should make our lives unfold according to our will.

We live in a world where we buy into the notion that we can—and have to!—have the whole thing planned and figured out. We lord it over our lives, and even our prayers, assuming that if we exert enough control over people, places, things—and God—we can maneuver them to our liking. Motherhood is one of the great gifts God has given to us to teach us that this is simply not true. It helps us conform ourselves to the reality that we are not in control and facilitates us learning the truth that God is in control. Further, it teaches us that we are not masters of our lives or the lives of others but rather called to be attentive servants to the good plans God has for us. We, like Mary, are called to be *handmaids* of the Lord and of his splendid plans, to which we are invited to say yes.

So, what exactly is this handmaid that Mary calls herself? Twice, Mary uses the word *handmaid* in Luke's gospel, both when giving her consent to the greatest announcement ever made (1:38) and when proclaiming her beautiful Magnificat to her cousin Elizabeth (1:48). In calling herself "handmaid," Mary identifies herself as a bondmaid of the Lord, as one bound as closely to God as a slave to its master. Mary is God's bondservant because she understands her utter dependence on him and she trusts in his power over her. Mary, who had the most intimate experience of God's personal presence and power ever manifested to a human being, describes that power to Elizabeth with the words "greatness," "holy," "mercy," "might," and "help" (1:46–55). She knows that God can be relied upon to provide all that she needs, and it is clear to her that God, and not she, is in charge.

Control Versus Surrender

Frankly, admitting that we are not in control is a profoundly countercultural message today, even in the Christian church. "Helicopter parenting" has become "helicopter Christianity," and we find ourselves inundated by the message that if we think, do, and pray all the right things, we'll be guaranteed that our lives will go well. We buy into the message that we can have an assurance of a life that is full of only blessing and abundance, and then we find ourselves befuddled and despairing when our lives hit the skids.

One of the most popular books ever written on the prayer of Christian mothers, selling thirty million copies worldwide, emphasizes making extensive lists of every aspect of our children's lives—listing everything we could possibly think of or imagine, even a year into the future— so we can cover every area in prayer, leaving nothing out. Focusing on *our* power, the book promises that if mothers pray hard enough and biblically enough, we can orchestrate the release of blessing into the lives of our children, sparing them loss and harm. The author even makes the audacious claim that during all the years that she and her prayer group covered their children in this type of prayer, they "never lost a single child—not to disease, accident, rebellion, ungodliness, or to the enemy's plans."[1]

What planet were they living on, I wonder?

Let's be completely honest: Who doesn't wish there was a guarantee that if we pray a certain way, our children's lives will be full of blessing and prosperity, and free from harm? I certainly do! But this type of approach to prayer, also known as the "prosperity gospel," inadvertently turns prayer into a formula for success, a magical method that portends to enable us to control the outcomes of our children's lives and the world around us if we pray enough or do it just the right way. No wonder the book was so darn popular!

Such magical thinking does not line up with reality, and it's certainly not congruent with the message of Christianity, which is the message of the Cross. Furthermore, it doesn't line up with the life of Mary, the most blessed woman that ever lived, who watched her Son suffer a brutal, violent death upon the Cross. Mary's most exquisite blessing was not that she was given a "pass" on suffering but that she was permitted to participate in the Cross in a most profound and intimate manner. She found the greatest blessing precisely by uniting her deepest agony— watching her Son die upon the Cross—to her Son's own sacrificial offering, cooperating freely with salvific grace in bringing about the redemption of souls. We are invited to do the same whenever the Cross presents itself in our lives, turning our pain into a source of sanctification for ourselves and for others. It is thus that we "rejoice in our afflictions" (Rom 5:3; Col 1:24).

So, does embracing the Cross mean we shouldn't pray for our children, or that we should fatalistically accept whatever life sends, without asking God for miracles, conversions, and cures? Such an extreme position would be folly and, if true, would eliminate the need for another book about prayer. Jesus instructs us to pray and to present our needs to him with boldness, persistence, and confidence (Mt 7:7; Mt 21:22; Jn 14:14).

While there is no cookie-cutter recipe for making life happen according to our prayers, we can and do see miraculous answers to prayer all the time, even when our prayers aren't answered in exactly the way we hoped or asked for. Thus, it is important to begin to behold the deeper miracles that happen when we pray, such as the miracle of learning to trust God and capitulate to him, resting in the knowledge that he loves us tenderly and particularly. Or perhaps we can appreciate the miracle of seeing the events in our lives through the eyes of *faith*, wherein we are given the supernatural ability to participate in God's own understanding, which sees this life for what it really is: a preparation for heaven and an opportunity to embrace human and divine love.

One of the most powerful answers I've ever received to prayer was the incredible conversion of my late husband, Bernie, for whom I'd prayed fervently for twenty-five long years. My many prayers for Bernie's conversion were answered in a way that was totally unexpected and unasked for—via his massive heart attack, near-death experience, and personal meeting with God in heaven. Bernie awoke from a six-week coma to communicate to me the details of his God encounter, telling me repeatedly, "You have no idea how much God loves you." He also spoke the sweetest words I'd ever heard him say: "I surrendered to God. . . . I have so much peace."

I spent the next six weeks by his side in the ICU praying doggedly for his physical healing and return home, believing we would together go into ministry just the way I'd always dreamed, sharing the message of God's profound love he had received on the other side. It wasn't until the very end of Bernie's life that I embraced the truth that he had received from God exactly the healing he needed— the ultimate healing—which was to be readied for heaven and called to his eternal home. Though my prayers weren't answered in the way I had desired or requested, God used that experience of deep suffering and purification to teach me that he can be trusted and that he does not—cannot— abandon us. He used our journey through sickness and death for his good and merciful purposes, which included healing the wounds in Bernie's soul, and mine, in very different but necessary ways.

I learned through that experience that God's thoughts are not our thoughts and his ways are not our ways—but that, indeed, his ways are *good*. God's plans are often a mystery to us—a mystery to which we must simply bow. We can pray, ask, listen, and wait on the Lord, but ultimately we must, as Bernie and I both figured out, surrender to God in trust.

Motherhood Is the School of Surrender

We are raising our families in an age where moms often hover over their children and micromanage every aspect of their lives. But do we live in an age of faith-filled moms, a world of women on their knees allowing God to transform them and their children through the persistent offering of prayer? This book is meant to encourage women to do just that: to pick up the banner of prayer, to pray unceasingly, and to learn to surrender our children and ourselves to God.

One of the best compliments I've ever received came from my daughter Gaby, whose fourth child, Rose Grayson, was born on Holy Saturday. "I remember you were always on your knees, praying for us," she said recently while sharing about one of her little one's struggles. "I'm realizing that I've got to get more serious about praying for my children." What she doesn't know yet is just how powerful praying for her children will be and how much it will change her too.

Indeed, it is among a mother's most important labors to pray diligently for her children. And that doesn't always happen with words. Sometimes our prayers go forth through songs and dancing. Sometimes they rise up through tears and groans. But whatever form they take, the prayers of a mother's heart have to be one of the most potent forces in the universe, because they effect so much love in the world.

I think of my own mother as I write these words on the Feast of St. Jude, the day before my birthday. My mother always told me that she named me after St. Jude because she had the Asian flu when I was born, and she prayed a novena to "the patron saint of impossible causes" that God would spare my life. I firmly believe my mother's prayers not only saved my life but also ultimately led me to know, love, and serve God.

While I wandered far from God in college and temporarily lost faith in him completely after graduation, I found my way to a personal relationship with Jesus in an evangelical Christian church at the age of twenty-three. I now understand that conversion as the day my infant Baptism at Immaculate Heart of Mary Church in New Orleans finally "took." Five years later, Mary Immaculate grabbed hold of me and brought me back home to the church of my childhood, back to the bosom of the Catholic Church and the family table of the Eucharist. For the last twenty-seven years, she has led me along a path of ever-deepening conversion, helping me learn to say yes to God in all things—not just the things I find palatable or easy to swallow. Mary has revealed herself over time as my own heavenly Mother, a Mother who's led me to love her Son more deeply while teaching me the virtues of docility and obedience to Christ and his Church. Further, she has cradled me tenderly and unceasingly as multiple tragedies have struck our lives—as I buried my stepson, two brothers, and husband, and then came terrifyingly close to burying my firstborn son to addiction. The Blessed Mother is the ultimate model of femininity and motherhood, and I've looked to her constantly over the years both as an example of godliness and as a source of powerful heavenly intercession, particularly in my endeavors as a mother.

Motherhood has been one of the most rewarding, humbling, and enlightening undertakings of my life, and, oh, how I've needed Mary's help! It has made me love with reckless abandon and driven me countless times to my knees, begging for God's grace, mercy, and intervention. And I see no end in sight. *Because* I am a mother, I am a praying mother. And I will remain a praying mother all the days of my life.

I invite you to join me now on this journey in prayer through the life and heart of Mary, the Mother of God. May we see tremendous fruit in our lives and in the lives of our children as we pray through the forthcoming chapters of this book. And may Mary, Mother of divine grace and treasure house of God's graces, pray for us.

Making Space for Love

PONDER

How hard is it for me to surrender my children or myself to God? How attached am I to the belief that I am in control or that I have to hold on to specific outcomes for things to be okay? What would happen if I released everything completely to God's care, including my children? Am I willing to do that now?

PRAY

Father in heaven, I thank you for the gift of my children and for the sublime vocation of motherhood. I admit that I have often been full of fear, worrying endlessly about my children, about their lives, their futures, and their safety. Yet, Lord, you teach us that "there is no fear in love" and that "one who fears is not yet perfect in love" (1 Jn 4:18). Make your love perfect in me, Father, that I may live free of fear and full of faith and trust in you, especially regarding my children. I entrust them to you now, placing them into the Immaculate Heart of Mary and the Sacred Heart of Jesus, and into the safe embrace of your loving, merciful hands. Watch over them, Father. Hold them close to your heart at all times, guiding them safely to their eternal destiny with you in heaven. I relinquish control over their lives and their futures to you, surrendering them to your holy will. Father, help me to trust that you love them more than I, and help me daily to live in that trust. In Jesus' name I pray. Amen.

Chapter 1

HE ANNUNCIATION:
THE YES OF SURRENDER

Fiat?

"I'm pregnant," I said tentatively over the phone to my dear friend Cecil, uncertain what her reaction would be. I was thirty-eight years old and my husband, Bernie, was fifty-four, after all. This was my fifth child and Bernie's seventh, and we'd long ago rid our house of baby stuff and baby dealings. What would people think? Additionally, with four other children ages eight to twelve in three different schools, and with me being enrolled in a full-time master's of theology program, I couldn't even begin to imagine how an infant would fit into the scheme of things. But I had said yes to God on this, and I would have to trust him to work out the details of our busy, high-octane lives.

"Hooray!" Cecil screamed at the top of her lungs over the news, her jubilation betraying all the years of stripping it took to get me to this place.

I had wrestled with so many noes as a woman, struggling to give my consent to all that womanhood and

motherhood demanded. Although one of the great desires
of my life was to be a wife and mother, I was surprised by
how much the vocation of family stretched me, by how
tired I was, and by how inadequate I often felt in front of
the task of loving hearts and shaping lives.

"I am not having any more children!" I had declared
at the age of thirty, getting on the pill when our youngest
child at the time, Christian, turned one. Though Bernie
would have had a vasectomy at the time, he was afraid to
go under the knife, so he happily threw the ball of man-
aging our fertility back into my court.

I'd returned to the Catholic Church at age twen-
ty-nine, and by thirty-five, I'd arrived at a juncture in my
spiritual journey where I had to make a decision about
whether or not to embrace all that the Church teaches,
including its instruction on regulating family size. It took
three years of intense soul searching and wrestling with
God for me to agree (I'm surprised that I don't have a per-
manent limp from that brawl), but I ultimately said no to
contraception and yes to natural family planning (NFP),
which the Church teaches is a moral means of regulating
fertility. Although one of the hardest nods I've ever had to
give, my acquiescence would set me on a new trajectory in
life, a path that included saying yes to God if he wished to
give us another child.

About four years into my yes to natural family planning, I finally mustered the courage to pray, "Lord, if you
want to give us another child, I'm open," reversing my
previous plea of, "Please, please, please, God, don't let me
get pregnant!" Though I'd been petrified at the thought
of having more children while my husband and I were

using contraception, my resistance softened over time as we began to practice NFP, and eventually, the thought of welcoming a new baby no longer struck terror in my heart. In fact, I began to embrace the idea. Two weeks later, I learned I was pregnant.

While God could have sent us a child earlier as we practiced haphazard and sloppy NFP for several years, he had graciously and mercifully waited for my consent. Like Mary's fiat, my yes had been called forth from my inmost being to bear new life, a yes that signaled permission for God to do with me as he wished.

And therein lies the crux of the matter. The central point of the Christian faith is not that we must get pregnant or give birth to children to be authentic women of God but that we must consent to what is perhaps even more difficult, that is, learning to say yes to him.

May It Be Done to Me (Lk 1:38)

Motherhood, probably more than anything else in life, teaches us to say yes. Indeed, there are a million and one yeses in motherhood, all of them held together in the tension of unspeakable love and piercing swords, both large and small: yes to carrying new life; yes to the physical discomfort of a rapidly changing body; yes to painful birth, tender scars, and sore breasts; yes to being unable to conceive; yes to miscarriage; yes to adoption; yes to a willful two-year-old, three-year-old, or teen; yes to indescribable love for a new baby; yes to caring for a sick child; yes to countless nights of praying for a reckless young adult; and yes to practicing repeatedly and then rejoicing over a first step and every first step thereafter.

I had always thought of motherhood as "doing" something, such as getting pregnant, bringing home a baby, loving and fashioning a little heart and soul, and forming and directing another's life. I now understand that motherhood is meant to "do" something to us: form and fashion us, awaken and enrich us, strip and heal us, and teach us to become women of prudence, patience, and perseverance, as it trains us constantly in the art of consent. Much like the practice of prayer, motherhood holds the potential to mold us into beings who are receptive to God and to others, into persons who become ever more capable of living a life-giving, love-expanding yes.

Mary is the icon of humanity precisely because she reveals to us how to say yes to God. She shows us what a profound effect authentic human surrender can have—both on us and on the world around us, giving us a window through which to see how divine activity is supposed to play out in human affairs. Mary illustrates for us in living color the way in which all human beings are purposed to relate to God, teaching us what it looks like to open our hands, hearts, and bodies to him to allow the divine presence to penetrate and transform us and the entire created realm.

Mary's life teaches us that we are meant to be actively receptive to God, to his grace and to his will. Active receptivity is the ability to at once surrender and receive. It sounds like an oxymoron, but it's not. We must actively surrender to God in order to receive what he has for us. Why? We must do so because surrender involves the critical gesture of opening our hands. Hands clamped tight, holding on to our will and our ways, leave no room for God's gifts.

The greatest gift ever given to mankind—the Redeemer, the God-man, Jesus Christ—came forth in response to the surrendered yes of a woman. Mary demonstrates just how pivotal our assent is and how imperative it is that we learn to hear and readily respond to the voice of God.

Hearing Well

Before we can say yes to God, we must be attuned to his voice. God speaks to his people, and he awaits our response. One of my favorite scripture verses is in the book of Isaiah, where the Lord says,

> No longer will your Teacher hide himself,
> but with your own eyes you shall see your
> Teacher,
> While from behind, a voice shall sound in your
> ears:
> "This is the way; walk in it,"
> when you would turn to the right or the left.
>
> ~Isaiah 30:20–21

This gives us a stunning picture of the kind of intimacy we're meant to have with God: God, walking right behind us, whispering in our ear, and instructing us as we move forward so we will not deviate from the path of life but will continue to move forward in his will. Would you like to have that kind of intimacy with God? The good news is that it's entirely possible through a personal, living relationship with him, a relationship that includes giving our very selves to him and grounding our lives in prayer that we may become intimate with him and familiar with the sound of his voice.

Clearly, this is the kind of relationship that Mary had with God. She immediately recognized the angel Gabriel as God's messenger and readily assented to God's invitation to conceive and bear his Son. Mary's concurrence with God's plan establishes the paradigm of faith for all human beings: we are called to hear God's living, personal Word—Jesus—spoken to us, into us. We are invited to believe in him, receive him, conceive him, and bear him to the world. In the annunciation, Mary gives us an image of true obedience, "the obedience of faith," which is the "graced capacity to 'hear' God and respond completely and without reservation,"[2] the obedience to which we are all called as Christians.

Sadly, we often reduce the concept of obedience to blind, dutiful submission to an imposing authority, sort of like marching to the orders of a drill sergeant. When we think of obedience this way, we miss its beautiful meaning, as well as its important connection to our walk with God. The word *obedience* comes from the Latin word *oboedire*, which means "to listen, or to hear." When we are obedient to God, we are responding to the lover of our souls who beckons us, calls us, pursues us relentlessly, and waits patiently for our consent. It is when we hear God in this way that we can wholeheartedly obey him, saying yes courageously to whatever it is he asks of us.

God Speaks

I like to joke that God speaks, and I sometimes listen. And it's true. God is constantly communicating his love and presence to us, but our ears can be so stopped up from the noise and busyness in our lives that it's nearly impossible to hear him.

Often God speaks in a tiny whispering sound, as he did with the prophet Elijah (1 Kgs 19:12). I believe that's the way God most commonly communicates to us, whispering his presence through creation, through the Church and its sacraments, and through the events and people he sends into our lives. It is the habit of prayer that equips us to tune into God's frequency and hear what he has to say. Dedicated quiet time with the Lord each day—whether by attending daily Mass, meditating on the scriptures, spending time in adoration before the Blessed Sacrament, or praying favorite devotional prayers such as the Rosary— equips us to hear God's voice, to hear him announcing his tender love and life-giving plans into our ears, hearts, and lives. The discipline of prayer is meant to engage us in a dynamic dialogue with God—a person who knows us individually and intimately and who loves us infinitely.

Though God usually whispers, once in a while he shouts. On a number of occasions in my life, God's voice has literally rung my ears as he gave me a directive about something, usually something important.

The call on my life to study theology came about by God speaking loudly and clearly to me. Though I was registered at the time to begin a master's of counseling program at a nearby university, God redirected my path to the study of theology on a moment's notice following a conversation I had with one of my best friends from high school; this girl happened to be the most devout Catholic I knew during our teen years.

Carol had gone off to college in the northeast, gotten married, had three sons, and divorced. Back in town for a visit, she shared over dinner one night about a pilgrimage she'd made to India, where she'd become "enlightened" and converted to Hinduism. I was shocked and grieved that someone who had loved Jesus as much as Carol did could have concluded that he was not God and was no more than a prophet or a good example. Adding insult to injury, I was utterly unable to defend the Christian faith as we conversed about what we believed and why. I cried the whole way home from dinner, determined never to find myself in that situation again.

First thing the next morning, I drove to our neighborhood Catholic bookstore to buy a book to help me defend my faith. I picked up Scott and Kimberly Hahn's *Rome Sweet Home* and felt compelled to buy it. Ten hours later I finished reading the book, and while closing the last page, I heard God speak a message in my spirit that shook me from head to toe: "Learn and defend the Catholic faith!"

There was no doubt in my mind that God had spoken to me, or that I was called to get a master's degree in theology, even though it had never crossed my mind before that moment to do so. Knowing only that I could not go back to our local Catholic university, where I had attended as an undergraduate and become agnostic due to the watered-down, deconstructed version of the Catholic faith presented there, I called my sister-in-law Hedy, completely perplexed.

"Hedy," I began, "you're not going to believe what just happened to me!" After listening to my story about dinner with Carol, reading *Rome Sweet Home*, and hearing

God tell me to learn and defend the Catholic faith, she could contain herself no longer. "This is incredible!" she erupted in surprise and excitement. "I just got a call five minutes ago from a friend who's bringing a satellite campus of the University of Dallas to our area, and he needs to sign up twenty-five people for the master's of theological studies program by *Friday* in order to get it started. Call him immediately!" she suggested urgently, as it was already Tuesday.

By Friday, I had withdrawn from the master's of counseling program and enrolled in the master's of theological studies program, and the rest, as they say, is history. I have spent the past sixteen years of my life teaching and delving deeper into Catholic theology, having found my passion and mission via a direct intervention by God.

Hearing God's voice that day in my bedroom was a life changer for me, another yes God asked of me that set me on a new path that, while totally unexpected, has been immeasurably fulfilling. What might God be saying to you at this moment in your life? What yes may he be asking of you?

Yes, Seventy Times Seven

Once we begin to be attuned to God's voice through a relationship with him and through prayer, how often must we say yes to him? In how many ways must we learn to surrender? One? Seven? Seventy times seven? As Mary's life reveals, saying yes to God is a continual practice, a habit of the heart and mind that stretches us in the art of assent to God's will. The practice of this habit, which opens us up to God's life, love, and blessings, will be ongoing this side of heaven. The good news is that life gives us ample opportunities to practice this skill, and God gives abundant grace to respond, "Yes." The downside is that surrender can be "hawd," to use my mother's favorite New Orleans slang expression, especially when it involves suffering.

The word *surrender*, which comes from the Old French word *surrendre*, literally means to "give oneself over," or to "give back." What, exactly, are we giving back? We are giving back to God our lives and our very selves, recognizing that we are not our own and that we belong to him. As such, it is right and good to give ourselves over to God.

To surrender ourselves totally to the living God is to let go of all that we grasp for and hold in our hands. That includes our souls, our lives, our wills, our ways, our dreams, and . . . our children. Ouch! Such surrender opens the way for receptivity—the ability to receive the good things that God has for us and to trust that all that he permits in our lives is for our good. Just like Mary's, our surrender is manifested through—and contingent upon—our yes. God always honors our freedom and our right to say no.

It is important to realize how difficult it can be to say yes to God and that surrendering to him does not always mean that our life goes well—at least as the world defines "well." In fact, it is often when our life is not going as we expected that we learn to release ourselves fully to God. This involves learning to trust God—coming to believe that he is a loving, kind Father who guides our lives with tender providence, providence that is meant for our good. When we believe and begin to experience this to be true, we develop confidence that God is always acting mercifully on our behalf, and we rest assured that all will be well in our souls, no matter what life brings. True surrender brings our souls the fruit of peace that surpasses understanding and even the inexplicable gift of experiencing joy right in the midst of suffering. This is precisely the grace God wishes to give us, grace that enabled a father who had just lost his four daughters in a shipwreck to pen the following lines: "When peace, like a river, attendeth my way / When sorrows like sea billows roll / Whatever my lot, Thou has taught me to say / It is well, it is well with my soul."[3]

Surrender and the Sword

Surrender, while necessary and extremely liberating, can be very painful. That's because it often involves letting go of our plans, programs, and perceptions, while learning to rely on God with the confident expectation that he loves us and will work all things together for our good. The opportunity for such relinquishing is constantly at hand in life, especially in the life of a mother, and it can present itself in a myriad of different ways. These might include having a gaggle of less-than-perfectly spaced children, dealing with the heartbreak of infertility, or perhaps confronting a teen's strong rebellion or a child's serious illness. Or, as Mary's life demonstrates, and as I've witnessed personally in the lives of numerous women whom I love, it may involve the heartbreak of burying one's spouse or one's beloved child, both of which Mary sorrowfully did.

Every yes to God, including (and maybe especially) the painful ones, has become a portal for deeper intimacy with him. Each surrender has helped me to abandon

myself to God in more life-giving ways, to die to my will,
my ways, and my whims, and to come alive to him. Each
time I've given God my assent, he's met my yes with
grace—grace to love and trust him, grace to believe he is
good (it can be hard to believe God is good in the midst of
intense suffering), and grace to keep walking forward in
faith. Each yes offered to God from the heart makes more
space for more of his love, cracking our hearts open that his
love may enter us more deeply, that we may hold more of
it, and, yes, that we may transmit more of that sweet love
to others in this all-too-broken world.

We are often given the opportunity to practice the yes
of surrender through the vocation of motherhood, which
affords us countless occasions for our heart to break open
and for us to learn to let go and let God. Motherhood challenges us to deeply embrace the truth that God is a loving,
merciful Father—a Father who loves and cares for our children infinitely more than we can imagine and infinitely
more than we are capable of loving them ourselves.

Life and Death Annunciations

"It's a boy!" my husband, Bernie, beamed as he carried
our white-haired, blue-eyed, nine-pound newborn out into
the hall of the hospital, where thirty family and friends
awaited his arrival on September 2, 1999.

"Hooray!" a loud shout went up from the hall, to
which my doctor looked at me genuinely perplexed and
said, "I've never seen a family so happy over the birth of
a fifth child!"

I was elated beyond words as I held a perfect infant
in my arms, and as I looked into his lovely little face, I

wondered, "What in heaven's name was I so afraid of?" I could no longer remember why the thought of having another child had been so frightening to me. In fact, all I could think about from the first moment I laid eyes on Benjamin was how much I loved him—how much we all loved him.

Our daughters, who were thirteen, twelve, and ten at the time, gladly assumed the role of Benjamin's "second mothers," and they quickly learned to bathe, change, dress, and rock him, as well as to slather him down with lotion so he smelled perfectly delicious. Thankfully, I was nursing the child, because feeding times proved to be the only time I didn't have to fight the kids to hold him if one of them, including our nine-year-old son, Christian, was in the house.

We joked throughout Benjamin's infancy and young childhood that he was "well loved"—the only thought that brought me any consolation when I came home on a dreary, cold March morning in 2009 to tell him his daddy had died. In all of the many times we thought we were losing Bernie during his eighty-seven-day ordeal in the ICU, my heart ached most over the reality that our son might lose his father.

The memory of breaking the news of Bernie's death to Benjamin is forever seared into my memory, as is the recollection of our precious baby boy climbing into the hospital bed to cling to the body of his frail, dying father and beg God for his daddy to live. "Please God, have mercy" was all I could pray as I thought of the trauma Benjamin would experience losing a parent in childhood, not to mention the pain of remembering his father beset by the effects of congestive heart failure that had left Bernie, and his entire body, in a state of unmitigated decompensation.

I learned the hard way that I could not spare Benjamin or my other children the loss of their father—or any other suffering in life, for that matter. But I could ask for the grace to show them what it means to live in a posture of surrendered acceptance to God's will for our lives, and teach them that God's got this, and he's got us too.

There were plenty of tears and much hard grief after Bernie's death, and I felt totally disoriented for a while by the unforeseen course upon which we were now traveling. Even so, remembering Benjamin's eyes as they scanned my face for reassurance when he learned of his father's death convinced me I had a choice about how I would handle the suffering that had visited our lives. Would I let the suffering we'd endured break through my heart and change me? Would I let its flame transform me, making me soft, luminous, and more loving? Would I allow the fire of suffering to burn away the dross in me that had cast shadows on my life thus far—the focus on myself and my own needs, the turning in on my own pain, and the inability to love for love's sake alone, and not for love's payoff? I was acutely aware that I was at a crossroads in dealing with the anguish life presented: I could turn toward the Cross and let its fruit bleed life into me or turn away from the life-giving seeds the Cross yields, letting them escape me completely. I, like Mary, had to choose.

Mary walked headlong from the annunciation to the foot of the Cross, her yes to God not exempting her at any point in the journey from the pain of life's suffering. Not immune to travail and loss, Mary willingly participated in a unique and heretofore unheard of manner in giving them an entirely new, grace-filled meaning—cooperating with Jesus in transforming suffering into a gateway of healing and purification, and death into the doorway to eternal life and unending bliss. She allowed the sword's sharp tip to lance her heart wide open, letting her Immaculate Heart become a sacred door of life, love, and grace, just as we are invited to do.

Making Space for Love

PONDER

What yes might the Lord be asking of me right now in life? What am I most afraid to say yes to, or most afraid to let go of? Can I open my heart and hands to the Lord, asking him to help me trust him more deeply?

PRAY

Lord Jesus, sometimes I find it so hard to pray, "Thy will be done." I ask for the courage and humility to open my hands to you and to surrender my will to yours. Open my ears, Lord, that I may clearly hear the sound of your voice and discern your plans and purposes for my life. Give me the grace to be obedient, to hear well, and to respond quickly when you call my name. Please grant me the grace of trust, especially when suffering visits my life. Son though you were, you learned obedience through what you suffered, surrendering yourself on the wood of the Cross out of love for me. May I say yes to surrendering to you and to embracing the Cross, expecting you to give me life through the infinite merits of your all-redeeming

death. Help me to trust that you love me infinitely, that
you are good, and that you work all things together for
my good, my sanctification, and my salvation. Lord, I ask
for a spirit of acquiescence like your holy Mother, that I
may say yes to you in all things, even when I am disap-
pointed, sorrowful, or afraid. Make yourself known in my
yes, Lord, and may I rest in the knowledge that my yes,
united to yours, can only bring forth life. I ask for life in
abundance, for me and for all those I love. In your holy
and precious name I pray. Amen.

Chapter 2

HE VISITATION:
THE POWER OF GODLY FRIENDS

A true friend is more loyal than a brother.

~Proverbs 18:24

Mothers need friends. We all need friends. Boy, have I *ever*
needed friends, especially when life's gotten hard.

Many times, we forge friendships around our children; we build lasting friendships *because* of our children—becoming friends with the parents of our children's
friends, who over time, soccer games, ballet recitals, and
school dances become our dearest friends. The seasons of
friendship in our lives often revolve around the seasons
of growth in our children's lives. And I'm sure that's how
it should be.

I was closing in on thirty-nine when Benjamin was
born. Most of my friends had ceased having children by
then, and I fretted about who would be there to play with
him, to love him and fight for him as a brother, knowing

how insanely important my children's friends were to them, and their mothers to me.

During my pregnancy, I began to pray that God would send Benjamin a friend. One afternoon when I was about seven months' pregnant, I was on my knees planting the garden in front of our home and praying to St. Thérèse of Lisieux to help my flowers thrive. Suddenly, a car appeared before my eyes, stopping right in front of the brand-new house newly under construction across the street. Out stepped Michelle, looking young, fresh, and about five months' pregnant. We introduced ourselves, and I learned that she was my new neighbor and the answer to my prayers. Our boys, Benjamin and Matthew, were born eight weeks apart. I adopted Michelle as my little sister, and she adopted Ben as her second son. "Benja-Jo" and "Matt-man" have been joined at the hip ever since. Now gangly sophomores in high school, they're growing like weeds, and we joke about how, before we know it, they'll be standing in each other's weddings. There's nothing like a lifelong friend.

Who (but God) knew just how much Ben would need a best friend right across the street as we faced the immense crisis of Bernie's illness and death and as our house emptied out and we said good-bye to most of its inhabitants in the course of a few short years? Ben was just nine when Bernie died, and within a year all four of our older children, including Kara and Alexandra, who had returned home for an extended time during Bernie's illness, departed our home too. In one fell swoop, our house went from being a bustling center of activity for a family of seven to the dwelling of a single, widowed mother and a frightened, fatherless little boy. The silence in our home was deafening, and thankfully, Benjamin found refuge in Michelle's busy, noisy home. Matthew was a welcome, steady presence in Ben's life during that sorrowful time in our lives, and hearing their voices happy at play in the empty lot across the street reassured me there was still some normalcy in life, that life would resume its course eventually, and that someday we would find our ground again.

I Have Called You Friends (Jn 15:15)

It is said that real friends are worth their weight in gold, and how true it is. A good friend will love us, bless us, challenge us, speak the truth to us, and reveal the Truth to us. A friend brought me to that little evangelical Christian church in New Orleans, where I gave my life to Christ. Another friend led me back to the Catholic Church and, through her example and encouragement, helped reintroduce me to the Blessed Mother, who eventually became my own friend.

Jesus tells his disciples that he no longer calls us slaves but friends. Why? Because he has told them everything he has "heard" from the Father (Jn 15:12–17). And what is the message of the Father? It is *love*. Jesus reveals to his disciples in flesh and blood the love of God, and he commands us to extend that same love to one another. Thus, a true friend will not only love us but also reveal God's love to us.

This is the dynamic we see between Mary and her cousin Elizabeth at the visitation. Immediately after the annunciation, Mary hastens to travel nearly one hundred miles to visit her older pregnant cousin to love her, care for her, and share the good news of Christ with her. Mary's very presence brings with it a revelation of the incarnate love of God, Jesus, whose divine person is instantly recognized by both Elizabeth and the child within her womb (Lk 1:44). The holy friendship of Mary and Elizabeth establishes a prototype for all Christian friendships, which are meant to bring a tangible extension of the love of God and the presence of Christ into the realm of human relationships.

Somehow, as a Protestant evangelical, I had bought into the notion that a friendship with Mary and, in fact, practically any mention of her name, was anathema, as the Blessed Mother would supposedly lead me away from Jesus. It took me several years to overcome both my prejudice against Mary and my fear of welcoming her into my life. But thanks to the persistence of a few good friends, Mary, the Mother of God and model of true friendship, eventually found a place in my heart and my home.

Wherever You Go I Will Go (Ru 1:16)

When Bernie and I first married, I had been attending a little evangelical church called University Christian Fellowship (UCF) for about a year and a half. I was going nowhere near the Catholic Church at the time, so he, a nonpracticing Catholic, agreed to attend church with me. The first day we walked into UCF, Bernie recognized a friend he had known in high school, who happened to have the same first name and birthday as him.

"Bernie?" I heard him ask a man who was standing next to his wife in the pew on the right side of the old building.

"Bernie!" I heard the man respond exuberantly.

The smiling Bernies introduced their wives to each other, and Pat and I became instant friends. Pat soon invited me to join a weekly prayer meeting at her house, where a group of about ten women and their nursing babies gathered for praise and worship and spontaneous prayer; this was a group that my firstborn baby, Kara, would soon join. One of the ladies in the group, who had been a backup singer for Christian recording artist Amy Grant, taught us many beautiful praise and worship songs, which I sang to Kara every night as we rocked. (Remember the colic story? I sang to Kara for hours every night. I remain convinced that planted the seed for her to eventually become a Christian singer.)

The time spent with that group of women was a wonderful season of budding friendship and fellowship, and the beginning of a faith journey together that would lead both Pat and me back into the Catholic faith. Ultimately, it would also lead us to the foot of the Cross with Our Lady, as Pat buried her twenty-nine-year-old daughter, Ashley, following a car accident, and I buried my Bernie seven years later.

It all began when my sister-in-law, Hedy, invited me to her home in Pearlington, Mississippi, to pray a Rosary and hear a presentation about a Marian apparition. I invited Pat, also a former Catholic, to go with me, and we spent much time in the ensuing months discussing whether or not Mary could lead us away from Jesus. We were genuinely terrified of being deceived, and while it seems laughable now, only someone who's been convinced that Marian devotion equals idolatry can fully understand

how scared we were of offending God by having any kind
of relationship with Mary. We began to pray for God to
show us the truth about the Blessed Mother, earnestly
seeking to learn if God would send her from heaven with
messages for his people, as the Church claims he did at
Lourdes, Fatima, Guadalupe, and other apparition sites.
We read several books and hashed things out endlessly, all
the while asking God to show us the truth.

A turning point came when Pat, who arose at the
crack of dawn each morning to read the Bible and pray for
several hours (one of the things I still love about her to this
day), saw something "new" when reading Revelation 12, in
particular verses 5 and 17, which say, "[The woman] gave
birth to a son, a male child, destined to rule all the nations
with an iron rod. . . . Then the dragon became angry with
the woman and went off to wage war against the rest of her
offspring, those who keep God's commandments and bear
witness to Jesus." While Protestants primarily interpret
"the woman" as the Church, Catholic exegetes have always
seen a dual layer of symbolism in the passage, interpreting
"the woman" as Mary as well. Suddenly, the light came
on for Pat. I can still hear her voice over the phone telling
me excitedly, "Mary is the woman who gave birth to the
male child. . . . It says *her offspring*, and that makes us *her
children*. She is our Mother! As if our Mother would lead us
away from her Son, Jesus!" 'Nuff said. The question was
settled for her, and she returned to the Catholic Church.

I watched Pat return but was not completely convinced. Besides the issue of contraception, Mary was the
biggest stumbling block for me when considering coming back to the Catholic faith. I simply could not fathom

how having a relationship with both Jesus and his Mother would not somehow take my attention away from him. I was deeply conflicted, but I could not deny that Pat was growing more in love with Christ. I desired to have what she'd found, as Pat shared with great joy and enthusiasm all that she was learning about the Blessed Mother and the Catholic faith. We had become such deeply connected friends that I wanted to continue to share both the love and worship of Jesus with her. But, honestly, did that have to include Mary? Our discussions continued, but it wasn't until I heard Our Lady speak directly to me that I turned the corner myself and came home.

How Does This Happen to Me, That the Mother of My Lord Should Come to Me? (Lk 1:43)

Many times I prayed for God to show me the truth about Mary. One evening, in desperation, I prostrated myself on the floor, a prayer posture the evangelicals I knew assumed when they were really serious about something. I prayed, "God, if this thing about Mary is from you, then you have *got* to show me!" That prayer held the same degree of ardency as the one I'd prayed as an agnostic college graduate, when I begged God to show me if he was real. It was then that God revealed himself powerfully and personally to me, and I have never doubted his reality for an instant since. Don't ask me why, but God seems to specialize in promptly answering such fervent cries of the heart.

That night as I lay sleeping, I was awakened by what sounded like the door of my bedroom clicking open. I then heard a woman's voice pierce the darkness, saying, "I will cleanse your family." I sat up in bed to see if Bernie, who had fallen asleep watching TV on the sofa, had entered the room. Realizing I was still alone, my heart began to race. I lay awake for the rest of the night wondering what I had heard, believing it to be the voice of the Blessed Mother bringing a message from God. Did it mean that Our Lady's intercession would bring healing and conversion to my family, for which I had been praying for years? That made a lot of sense to me, but I was doubly frightened now about the prospect of being deceived.

The next day I prostrated myself again on the floor, pleading with God to confirm if the message had been from heaven. As I prayed, the phone in the kitchen began to ring, and I got up from the floor to answer it. On the other end of the line was my younger brother Kenny, who had moved to Florida months earlier and to whom I had not spoken since.

"Judy," he began. "I wanted to tell you that I was walking down the beach and an old Catholic man came up to me and asked if I'd ever accepted Jesus Christ as my personal Lord and Savior. I knelt down on the beach and prayed to receive Christ," he continued. "I don't know why, but I felt the need to call and tell you that." His words were music to my ears, in language that was all too familiar to me as an evangelical Christian.

I immediately began weeping so hard that I had to hang up the phone. Unbeknownst to Kenny, I had been asking God for a sign at the very moment he called, and the specific sign I was looking for to confirm the "cleansing" the Blessed Mother had promised was the conversion of my family members. God knew that I, a skeptic about Mary, would need a dramatic answer to prayer to be convinced of her intercessory role in our lives. I returned to the Catholic Church that week and have never looked back.

Am I delusional for insisting that I heard Our Lady's voice that long-ago night in my room? Call me crazy, but I can only say that I have never doubted the experience for a second. Mary's intervention that night has brought forth abundant fruit in my life, including an increase of faith and a deeper love of Jesus and his Church. It produced in me a yearning for the sacred, which would ultimately manifest itself in a love of the liturgy and its summit, the Eucharist. Further, Mary's visitation kick-started the years-long process of healing my conception of the feminine, both in the world and in myself. Her love, example, and intercession softened in me the rough edges of a silent but seething rage toward men, formed by a conglomeration of wounds that included childhood sexual abuse; the influence of a generation of angry feminists who viewed men primarily as "male chauvinist pigs"; and years of soul-fracturing sexual promiscuity as a young adult that was supposed to liberate me.

It was as though Our Lady came to take me by the hand and bring me on a journey through her own heart, to befriend me and show me a new way to be a woman—a woman in her very own likeness. Though it will take the rest of my life to unpack the words "I will cleanse your family" and receive what they proclaim, I now know that the important work of purification began within me upon Mary's visit, specifically with an interior revolution in the concept of womanhood as I knew it.

I learned, and continue to learn, that I don't need to clench my fists at men or at God in order to live in this world. I now understand that to be a woman is not simply a choice between being a man slammer or a doormat but rather a doorway—a gateway to life, love, and beauty. For so long I believed that my survival as a female meant living in a defensive posture against real or imagined male domination—including God's. Mary's influence untied that convoluted knot in me, prompting a paradigm shift. I came to see that to be a woman, a mother, and a bride— in a word, feminine—is to embrace the "masculinity" of God, a spiritual reality that turns this world's idea of the masculine on its head with its chief mark of self-donating, self-sacrificing love. I am more aware than ever that the great dragon ferociously wants to "sweep her away with the current" (Rv 12:15), for Mary is the iconic representative of vulnerable trust in God; she is a sign par excellence of self-yielding to the source we call Father, the one who alone can give life.

Needless to say, Mary's presence in my life had profound implications, and I was soon aware that it prompted me to change. Would I imitate the posture of Our Lady— the Woman—with hands, heart, and body surrendered completely to God? Would I let my conception of myself, especially in relation to the masculine, be transformed? And would I join her at the foot of the Cross to learn how to live—and die?

Standing by the Cross of Jesus [Was] His Mother (Jn 19:25)

My friend Pat had moved from New Orleans to North Carolina several years earlier, and my bags were packed to leave for the Carolina beaches. There, an extended group of family (she's one of thirteen children!) and friends would assemble to celebrate her fiftieth birthday. It was going to be a blast! Though Pat's birthday had come and gone on September 3, her party would coincidentally be celebrated the week of my October birthday, a double celebration for us. The phone rang at eight in the morning, just as I was preparing to leave to teach a class, before heading to the airport.

"Judy, it's Joe," the voice on the other end said, identifying the husband of Cynthia, Pat's best friend in her new hometown of Asheville. "I'm sorry to have to call and tell you this, but Ashley was killed in a car accident last night." With those horrifying words, I was now going to the funeral of Pat's eldest child, Ashley, who would be buried on my birthday.

The funeral Mass was held at the stunning Basilica of St. Lawrence in Asheville, North Carolina, one of thirty-three basilicas in the United States. Pat asked me to read, and I prayed that I could get through it without breaking down. Walking through the basilica's front doors, I was cut to the core by the life-size woodcarving of Christ mounted on the Cross right behind the main altar. But what took my breath away was the life-size sculpture of Our Lady standing beneath her dying Son, head tilted up, hands open and turned upward in surrendering prayer.

As Pat and her family processed into the church, it was devastating to see my friend, whom I loved so dearly, walking beside her beloved daughter's coffin. Her frail body, her grief, and her embodied pain created a stunning visual image of Our Lady in her deepest sorrow. Pat and I had talked many times about the symbolic meaning in Catholic architecture, particularly how the dome of a basilica is meant to give a sense of being in the womb of both the Church and of Mary. Now, here we stood, gathered in Mary's womb, grieving the death of Pat's child.

Pat had been the first friend I'd called when I learned of the suicide of my thirty-five-year-old brother, Scott. I had called her several times that week to ask her to pray for Scott, as I was sure he was in dire straits, drowning in the abyss of drug addiction. Praying on the deck in our backyard on an exquisitely crisp, flawless May morning, I heard the phone ring in the kitchen. "Judy, I'm sorry to have to call and tell you this," my brother Kenny sobbed. "Scott just shot himself. He's dead." With six short words, the day went black. I called Bernie to come home immediately and then called Pat, wailing through the phone with grief and shock. I can still hear her sweet voice consoling me tenderly, repeatedly saying, "Oh, Judy, I'm just so sorry."

I kept my eyes on Our Lady throughout Ashley's funeral Mass, as she stood in soul-piercing surrender at the foot of her Son's Cross. I wept for Ashley, for Pat, for my own mother, and for Scott. Yet this time, there were no words heard—only the groans of a mother.

He Who Is a Friend Is Always a Friend, and
a Brother Is Born for the Time of Stress (Prv 17:17)

Seven years later, Pat offered to come stay with me after Bernie's funeral, to meet me in my grief. "I'll wait until the activity settles and everything gets quiet in the house," she shared from experience; "that's when it gets really hard."

"What can I do to make you feel better, my dawlin'?" Pat asked after her arrival, using the familiar New Orleans endearment with which we always address each other.

"Will you replant the gardens in my courtyard so I can have my refuge back?" I replied, unsure if it was too much to ask.

"Sure, my dawlin'," Pat graciously responded. "I'd be happy to do that for you."

For the next four days, I sat on the outdoor sofa watching my friend labor for hours on end to make our courtyard, one of my favorite spots on earth, lovely and tranquil again. Bernie had built the enclosed garden, with its brick walls, ornate wrought-iron fences, and soothing center fountain, because I wanted a place to pray. It was lifeless and haggard looking after the three bitter winter months spent with Bernie in the ICU, and I was too exhausted and weak to replenish it, though it was normally something I would love to do.

Not only did Pat put in numerous new plants, but she also brought in an entire truckload of dirt that was delivered to the front lawn, wheelbarrow by wheelbarrow, to freshen up the soil. I told her how I like to pray to St. Thérèse of Lisieux when I garden, and she nicknamed herself "The Big Flower." We laughed. She then painted

and erected the cypress shutters she found in our garbage
yard, which Bernie and I had intended to put on the house.
Hanging a large iron cross between them, she created a
sanctuary of new life, a place to begin again.

In a moment of searing grief, my old friend came back
to Louisiana for a visitation, bringing the ground of her
heart. Mature terrain, fertilized with her own blood, sweat,
and tears, mingled with plentiful drops falling from the
Cross, offered lovingly to God and to me.

Pat and I had found our way together as we sought
Mary's friendship, and she'd led us home to the Church.
We would make our way together again through the valley
of tears, only this time our home would be Mary's sorrowful heart.

Making Space for Love

PONDER

Can I remember a time in my life when God answered the
cry for a friend, for myself or for my child? What impact
has friendship made in bringing me closer to God? Have I
embraced Mary as my friend? Has her friendship brought
me closer to God and helped me better understand how to
be a woman in this world?

PRAY

Loving Father, thank you for the gift of friendship and for
the many ways friendship has positively affected my life
and the lives of my children. Thank you for the friends
you have sent to travel with us on this journey and for the
friends you still desire to give us. Father, please send holy

companions who will encourage us to always walk closely by your side. And may we be godly friends to those who seek our companionship and friendship, sharing the joy of faith in Christ as Mary and Elizabeth did. I entrust my family and myself in a special way to Mary and Elizabeth at the visitation, asking for the grace to share in the reverence and love they felt for Christ. May we, like Mary, carry Christ to others, and may we receive him in those you send into our paths with the welcoming embrace of love, especially those who may want us to stand with them at the foot of the Cross, when their hearts are pierced with suffering. In Jesus' holy name I pray. Amen.

Chapter 3

THE BIRTH OF JESUS: EMBRACING OUR POVERTIES AND OUR CHILDREN'S IMPERFECTIONS

The Crib or the Cross?

If you could choose, would you rather be present with Jesus and Mary at the side of the crib or at the foot of the Cross? For a long time, it was pretty much a no-brainer for me when I thought about that question—I'd always choose the crib. I wanted to be there for the moment in Jesus' life where the stars shone brightly, the animals cooed gently, and his parents knelt glowingly by the perfect Savior's side—instead of being a witness to the dark, violent, agonizing day of his death.

Now I understand that the Cross is inexorably connected to the crib. The crib points forward to the Cross, where Jesus will die for the sins of the world; the Cross is the crib's fulfillment, where the God-man, who was placed into a feedbox for animals at birth, is eaten alive for the sins of the world. You can't have the crib without the Cross. Both are the seedbeds of salvation, both point to utter poverty of spirit, and both demonstrate radical self-emptying and self-surrender to God.

My choice for the crib was driven by a romanticized version of the birth of Christ—a sanitized reading of that event that I also projected onto motherhood, where all would be warmth, joy, and glowing light. But that's not the reality of the crib. And it's certainly not an accurate picture of mothering children. Christ's crib, for all of its joy, innocence, and beauty, carries with it profound weight; it is a weight that puts the redemption of the entire created realm in the balance through the surrender of the God-man to utter powerlessness—powerlessness that I've felt so many times as a person and as a mother, powerlessness that has called me to surrender my life, myself, and my children to God.

The fact is, the crib and the Cross are one and the same reality; they are the wellspring of self-renunciating, self-sacrificing, vulnerable love. In both places, arms open wide to draw others into love, and in both, God empties himself out in love's abandonment. These images sum up the essence of motherhood, lived out most faithfully by the Mother of God.

When I reflect deeply about the life of Mary, I conclude it probably bears little resemblance to the childish tales we often conjure up in our heads. As the drama of the Incarnation begins, Mary is young and pregnant before living with Joseph and, therefore, suspected of adultery—a grave violation of the law punishable by stoning. She immediately finds herself in a relationship crisis when her betrothed wants to divorce her before the public marriage even takes place. She delivers her child far from home and removed from the comfort of the inn, placing her newborn in the only available bed, a dirty feeding trough for beasts. (Germ freak like me? Ugh!) Soon, she and Joseph are on the run, literally fleeing for the life of their infant Son, whom Herod wants to murder.

When she obediently presents her child to God in the Temple, she is assured that a sword will pierce her heart. Jesus is merely an infant, and the crib has already given birth to the Cross for his Mother. The next time she appears in the story, she's lost her Son for several frightening days as she and her extended family return home from Jerusalem, an event that foreshadows Jesus' three-day disappearance into the tomb upon his crucifixion. And these scenes from Mary's life encompass only the Joyful Mysteries!

What can we learn from Mary through all of this? Maybe we can learn that life is messy from the get-go and that God is always present in the midst of the mess. Perhaps we can learn that our own hearts will too be pierced so that their intricate, hidden thoughts may be revealed and redeemed. And maybe we will see that in the midst of great pain, we can stand at the foot of the Cross in faith, hope, and love, anticipating birth, new life, and a resurrection.

It wasn't long after I became a mother that I heard Our Lady's words: "I will cleanse your family." I had no idea at the time just how deeply those words would bleed grace into my life.

[Women] Will Be Saved through Motherhood, Provided [They] Persevere in Faith and Love and Holiness, with Self-Control (1 Tm 2:15)

One of the things I like to say to new, first-time mothers is, "Get ready to fall madly in love with your child. Nothing you've experienced yet in life is like the love you're going to feel as a mother." And it's true. There's nothing on earth quite like a parent's love for his or her child, an image that gives us a unique glimpse of God's tender, fierce love for us. Motherhood binds us to another human being in measureless, heart-enlarging ways. It can fill us with unspeakable joy and make us gaga with affection for the little person God has entrusted to our care, surprising us with its intensity and ardor—love so fervent that we feel the urge to eat our children up because we adore them so much.

What I don't say to new mothers, though it's equally true, is this: "Get ready to be surprised by the way motherhood will make you die a thousand deaths. Nothing you've experienced yet will make you suffer the way you will suffer as a mother." Motherhood gives us a unique glimpse of God's self-sacrificing love for us—love so intense it will prompt us to put our lives on the line to help or save our children. Furthermore, there's nothing like motherhood that has the potential to pierce our hearts, expose our wounds, reveal our masks, and humble us to the core. It is my belief that motherhood is meant by God for our healing, sanctification, and salvation. And heal us it will, if we let it.

I learned I was expecting our first child on Bernie's fortieth birthday—the same day my parents hosted our engagement party. I was excited to be pregnant after having anticipated the thrill of becoming a mother all my life, and our daughter, Kara, was loved, embraced, and wanted. Even so, the timing of my pregnancy left me feeling very embarrassed, especially since I'd given my life to Christ a year earlier and felt that I should have been able to live out the Bible's teaching regarding sex, which is sacred and reserved exclusively for marriage. Getting pregnant before marriage exposed the fact that Bernie and I had been engaged in sexual sin, lending itself to a sense of deep shame. The shame I felt was the beginning of my emotional unraveling and the start of a long journey of healing around both the wounds of my childhood and my relationship with God.

For me, the experience of becoming a mother was much like Lazarus being called forth from the grave, needing to be unbound. Being a fearful, anxious peacemaker in a chaotic, violence-prone family of ten children—a family where an angry, critical paternal voice set the tone in our home—I had rarely felt the emotion of anger before becoming a parent. For the most part, I had learned to survive in life by doing what was required of me, by staying out of trouble (or at least not getting caught), and by not feeling or demanding too much. I worked throughout high school and college, made decent grades, and generally did what was expected of me, without developing a strong sense of my own identity or much of my own voice. Getting married at twenty-four and having children was supposed to be the thing that would fulfill me at long last, a fulfillment that I believed would build on my fairly newfound relationship with Christ and make me "happy." Little did I know that the proverbial "doo-doo" was about to hit the fan.

I can see in retrospect that exposing our wounds, as well as the masks we form to hide them, is one of the great gifts God intends to give us through motherhood, a gift for which I am profoundly grateful. Motherhood is meant to make us more real, and I believe this to be the case for every one of us; even as I observe today, several new young mothers with whom I am closely connected begin to face their fears, control issues, and childhood injuries as they make the daunting leap into parenthood.

I still remember the shock of coming home from the hospital the day after Christmas, bringing with me a colicky baby that I could neither calm nor console for the first four months of her life. Besides my belief in Jesus Christ, the only thing I was completely convinced of in life was that I was going to be a great mother. Mere weeks into my new vocation, exhausted and discouraged, I became convinced instead that I was a complete failure.

My exhaustion mounted over the months as Kara's screaming intensified, and for the first time in my life, my anxiety flared to the point that I could not sleep at all, even though I had previously been famous for being able to sleep anytime, anywhere. I walked the floors through the nights, anxiously trying to figure out what I was doing wrong. Before long, my fatigue gave way to anger—an emotion that I had lots of exposure to in life but rarely ever felt.

Our second daughter, Alexandra, was born thirteen months after Kara, with Gabrielle and Christian following shortly thereafter. I didn't know a person could be so tired! With four children under five and a husband who worked in his own business from early morning until late at night, I was angry and overwhelmed most of the time, even though I hid it from those outside my home. While I appeared calm and competent in front of others, my emotions erupted when I was alone with Bernie or the kids, so much so that I began to be frightened by the level of rage I was feeling. When that happened, I decided to get some help, seeking out a Christian counselor who could assist me in working though the anger that seemed to be ruling, and ruining, my life.

I Will Restore You to Health; of Your Wounds I Will Heal You, Says the Lord (Jer 30:17)

The first counselor I saw asked me during the second appointment if I had been sexually abused as a child. "Yes, I was abused by a distant relative," I responded immediately, "but it didn't affect me at all." "Oh, right!" he was kind enough not to say. His question identified a core problem within me: an unresolved emotional wound that was wreaking havoc in my life—the effects of which came flying up to the surface in the face of becoming a mother, confronting my own deficits, and dealing with the stress of exhaustion.

I eventually moved on to a new Christian counselor, and the first day in her office she invited me to do a simple exercise. "Close your eyes and picture yourself as a little girl," she instructed; "then tell me what you see." Closing my eyes I saw a creature that looked like E.T. standing in a large tin garbage can, wrapped from head to toe in a snake. When I described the image to her, Nancy responded with sad eyes and asked, "How did your little girl get so dirty and evil?" I wept profusely that day and for weeks afterward over the internal image I had of myself, because I knew it was all too true. I was full of self-loathing and secretly felt damaged, tarnished, and unclean. I had never articulated those things to anyone, including God, but the mental picture I had of myself spoke a thousand words. I was in dire need of healing, and God, in his great mercy, wanted to grant me relief.

Over time, I came to understand that the trauma of abuse had left a festering wound within me, one that had deformed my self-image and left me emotionally fragmented, full of self-rejection, mistrust, and shame. I hid those inner realities beneath masks of calmness, competence, and people pleasing, even as my emotional turmoil and anger escalated to full-blown depression following the birth of our fourth child, Christian. It would take several years of both professional therapy and Christian healing prayer with a spiritual director for God to unravel the lies and distortions by which I was bound. Eventually, I began to learn to love myself, and after many years of struggle, I learned to trust God.

The process of acquiring radical trust in God came to a head when Bernie became critically ill. What I discovered when the bottom fell out of our lives is that in the midst of a worst-case scenario, God wants to show up in incredible, outrageous ways to demonstrate his unconditional love and faithfulness to us—just as he did when he delivered the Israelites from slavery in Egypt and led them through the desert to the Promised Land, and just as he did when he delivered mankind from the bondage of sin and death by dying on the Cross and rising from the dead.

I Will Save Your Children (Is 49:25)

So how did all this affect my children? And how did we eventually find healing? The truth is, my children sustained wounds growing up in our home, wounds that I still pray daily for God to heal and that I can see he has healed, is healing, and will continue to heal.

Thirty years and five children later, I've gained enough perspective to know and accept two important things. The first is that we live in a broken, sinful world, and we therefore all have wounds and baggage. Even Mary, who was given the unprecedented grace of being conceived without sin, living without sin, and giving birth to the sinless God-man, suffered immense pain due to the sins of this fallen world, pain that deeply wounded her Immaculate Heart. Whether we grow up with a critical, negative parent or experience the effects of a broken home, abuse, addiction, illness, or the death of someone dear to us, we suffer damage in this life through a myriad of different circumstances. This is simply a fact of life. And it's okay. The sins, limits, and deficiencies of this world are precisely what Christ came to redeem, and our hunger for wholeness and integrity points us to a loving God who longs to love and restore us, just as our longing for ultimate beauty, perfection, and bliss point us toward heaven, where sin, suffering, and death will definitively come to an end.

The second thing I've learned is that there is a God, and he is in the business of redemption and restoration! God is so much bigger than our faults and frailties, and he works through them to impart his presence to us and to those in our lives. Therefore, our wounds need not dismay or destroy us. In fact, they are the privileged portals through which grace, healing, and glory enter our lives— the very openings through which we can invite God to enter more deeply into our hearts. How is this possible? It is possible because it is often when our brokenness causes our lives to spin out of control that we turn to God for help, and it is then that we find him ready at hand to aid us. It is possible because, when we finally come face to face with our poverties, we can seek the face of a Father who is rich in mercy and kindness, a Father who wants our faces to glow with his radiant love, and not to blush with shame. It is possible because our limitations and failures can drive us to seek the strength of a God who is mighty, a loving Papa whose power is perfected in our weakness. The cracks in our hearts and lives thus become the place where Christ enters into our brokenness, offering the medicine of salvation for our sins, hurts, and ills, and calling forth our wounds and weaknesses to become a gift to others: glorified gashes in our humanity that impart compassion, mercy, and love to fellow suffering souls. This is how the drama of sin, redemption, and restoration plays out in our lives, and it's how we become Christ for others.

We can begin now to pray for our children to be healed of life's wounds, using the following prayer. I prayed this for each of my children at bedtime for many

years and believe it has brought many spiritual benefits
and blessings to them:

> Lord Jesus, I thank you for [child's name] and for
> the gift of his/her life. I plead in your precious
> blood over [child's name] and ask that you heal
> him/her from the moment of his/her conception
> until today. May you bless him/her and may your
> angels guard over him/her all the days of his/her
> life.

I then placed the child under the mantle of protection of
Mary, our heavenly Mother, and prayed a Hail Mary. I
closed by calling upon the intercessory power of St. Joseph,
the saint of each child's baptismal name, and other saints in
heaven with the simple invocation, St. Joseph, pray for us;
St. Catherine of Siena, pray for us; and so forth. Bedtime
prayers are the perfect time to teach our children to pray,
as well as to begin to pray for the healing of life's hurts.

He Who Sings Well Prays Twice (St. Augustine)

Most of us want to know how to effectively pray for others
and, yes, what it takes to get a miracle and receive healing
for ourselves and for our families. When I experienced my
adult conversion to Christ, the first way I learned to really
pray was through singing. Still an evangelical Christian at
the time of Kara's birth, I was exposed to beautiful worship music, which I sang to her as we rocked. I remember
those precious times worshipping God, and I know that,
even then, God was ministering his healing presence to
Kara and to me. It is no surprise that Kara would find such
consolation through music and that the gifts of singing and
songwriting, especially about her own personal struggles,

would ultimately be used mightily by God to touch the hearts of others with his medicinal love.

As Alex, Gaby, and Christian were born, we added many songs to our repertoire, and in due course, I acquired a guitar and learned to play all our favorite songs. Some of the happiest memories I have from that time in our lives are the many nights when I played the guitar after bath time, with the kids running around the living room singing praise songs and dancing with all their might. If their dad was working late, I would often play for another hour or two alone in the living room after putting the children to bed, and I remember well how God's presence filled our home and our hearts through praise. To this day sacred music remains for me a path of immediate access to God's presence. It also continues to play a significant part in the lives of my children, with our four eldest having sung in choirs or served as worship leaders at some point, and with our youngest son working hard on learning to play the guitar. I am now watching the next generation, my little grandchildren, learn praise songs from my daughter, Gaby. Even two-year-old Joseph yells "na, na" when they get in the car—a prompt for Gaby to put on his favorite song, which goes, "Every move I make I make in You / You make me move, Jesus. / Every breath I take I breathe in You. . . . Na, na, na, na, na, na, na."

I have developed a much deeper prayer life as I've grown older and had more available time to pray, and thankfully, I now have the luxury of "wasting" much precious time in prayer. But for young mothers who face long hours of caring for children with very little sleep, singing praise songs with your children and praying before meals and at bedtime are easy ways to begin to incorporate prayer into the rhythm of life. In recent years, we have developed the habit of praying a decade of the Rosary after supper, while the family is still seated together at the dinner table. This is a great time to teach children to offer petitions and prayers for others in need, as well as to each take time to offer thanks to God for the blessings he has bestowed upon us that day.

Let the Children Come to Me (Mk 10:14)

Kara, my Christmas baby, was an extremely precocious, intelligent, perceptive child—and a child with a very strong will that often clashed with mine. I saw a distinct change in her when she turned seven, the year she reached the age of reason. It seemed that she morphed from a defiant, emotionally charged child into a perfect angel overnight. She began to ask deep questions about God, wondering how a person gets to know him.

Besides praying with her, my advice was for her to simply pray and ask God to show her who he is, knowing that same prayer worked for me years earlier, albeit at a much older age. Several weeks after I told Kara this, she came back with the following frustrated report: "Mommy, I've been begging God to show me who he is, and he just won't!" That conversation began a long dialogue with Kara about God and faith, a conversation that continues to this day as she travels around the globe sharing her faith with others as a Christian singer, songwriter, and inspirational speaker.

I recently heard Kara share her testimony at a Magnificat women's ministry breakfast, and she reminded me of a talk we had when she was seventeen years old. As I said, Kara seemed to become a perfect child overnight, not only transforming from a challenging little girl to a very compliant one but also eventually becoming an outstanding student, singer, actress, chastity speaker, and community role model. At the end of her senior year, she had the lead role in the high school musical, just as she'd had during every year of high school. When Kara stepped out onto the stage in her costume, I gasped. I hadn't realized until then how thin she had become, and she looked as though she might literally break in half.

I began to notice that Kara was severely restricting her eating and that she carefully measured each bite of food she put in her mouth. One day in prayer, God showed me that Kara's outstanding performance in life was driven by the anxiety to measure up and that she felt she had to be flawless to win love and compensate for the anger, conflict, and mess she'd witnessed in our home. This role is known as the "family hero" in psychology books, and our oldest daughter had totally assumed the part of making our family look good. Sadly, she had done it with the full endorsement of Bernie and me, who were getting quite a charge from all her accolades.

After going to confession to repent of my part of what God showed me in prayer, I spoke to Kara about it one day in the kitchen. I can't remember all that was said, but I distinctly remember ending the conversation by saying to her, "You really believe you have to be perfect, don't you?" As Kara tells it, that was the moment the perfect image she had constructed shattered. Unable to keep the facade of perfectionism up any longer, she began to eat anxiously, suffer from panic attacks, and spin into a terrible emotional spiral. To make matters worse, two weeks after she left for college that August at the Catholic University of America, Bernie's eldest son and Kara's half brother, Marshall, died of sudden, unexplained liver failure at the age of thirty-six. Two weeks after that, we had to do an intervention on our almost-fourteen-year-old son, Christian, bringing him to a ranch in Wyoming to live for a year in the hopes of saving him from the destructive path he was on.

The tragedy of Marshall's death, combined with Christian's escalating problems, threw Bernie and me into a severe emotional and marital crisis, and both of us were barely able to function for months. Kara shared in her testimony that she felt she had lost two brothers and both of her parents all at once. Her whole world came unglued, and the emotional toll it took on her caused her to withdraw from Catholic University and ultimately complete her college degree online.

Ten years later, it is nothing short of miraculous to hear Kara share her own long journey toward healing, a journey that began when, in God's tremendous mercy, her mask of being a perfect person began to come undone. Her decompensation was the beginning of the recovery of her true self: a beautiful, godly woman who embraces her own poverties, wounds, and weaknesses and allows herself to be vulnerable to God and to others.

"One day in the chapel, I was crying and asking the Lord why I am so weak, fragile, broken," Kara disclosed in her testimony. "I heard the Lord say, 'Kara, the gift of Christmas is poverty. I made you a Christmas child, and poverty is your greatest gift.' That was a turning point for me," she shared. "Embracing my own poverty allowed God to fill me with his love and his joy."

This is precisely how Christ meets us in our wounds, hurt to hurt, pierced heart to pierced heart. He utterly identifies with our brokenness, and it is there that he offers comfort, consolation, and peace.

Blessed Are the Poor in Spirit, for Theirs Is the Kingdom of Heaven (Mt 5:3)

What does it mean to be "poor in spirit" so that the kingdom of heaven might be ours? To be poor in spirit implies that we are needy and insufficient and that we recognize ourselves as such. It means we are free from self-assertion and that we depend upon God and not on our own prowess to navigate this world with grace. It means that we let God be God so he might "grant [us] in accord with the riches of his glory" to "know the love of Christ that surpasses knowledge, so that [we] may be filled with all the fullness of God" (Eph 3:16, 19).

This is the paradox of the Christian walk, and it's what the crib and the Cross reveal: it is when we are weak that we become strong; when we are poor that we become rich; and when we die to ourselves, and to our preconceived notions of how life ought to be, that we at last find true life.

Mary's life incarnates par excellence what it means to embrace a spirit of poverty. The humble handmaid of the Lord, who knew not power, fame, or fortune, carried the fullness of God within her very being—secure in the knowledge that he alone is the font of true wealth and the treasure trove that confers the inheritance of God's kingdom.

Making Space for Love

PONDER

How have my poverties drawn me deeper to Christ? How has God used motherhood to heal the wounds of my heart? Do I trust the Lord to heal the wounds my own poverties or mistakes have inflicted upon my children? Do I trust God to be the perfect parent for them, especially in areas where I may feel I failed?

PRAY

Father in heaven, I thank you for the great gift of being a parent, for it is after you that every family on heaven and earth is named (Eph 3:14–15). Forgive me for the ways I have failed to represent your love to my children, just as I forgive my own parents for their sins, weaknesses, and failures. Bless my children, Father, with your infinite, merciful love and help them turn their faces toward you, their perfect Father in heaven. Heal their wounds and draw them into a personal encounter with you, for you love them and have counted every hair on their heads. You have carved their very beings into the palms of your hands. May my children make their way into the embrace of your fatherly love. Multiply the gifts and graces you have given them, Lord, and let your love make up for wherever mine was lacking. And may Mary our Mother in heaven lead us by the hand through the heart of her Son, Jesus, into your very own heart. It is there alone that we find rest for our souls, there alone that we find true life. In Jesus' holy name I pray. Amen.

Chapter 4

HE PRESENTATION:
THE PREVAILING POWER
OF THE DEDICATION

They took him up to Jerusalem to present him
to the Lord.

~Luke 2:22

I had no intention of baptizing our first two children when
they were born. Being an evangelical Christian at the time,
it didn't even cross my mind. I had come to believe that
only an adult profession in Christ mattered, or at the very
least, a confession of faith by a person who was old enough
to understand what he or she believed. Besides, I had been
taught that infants couldn't have faith in Jesus, so what
would be the point of having them baptized? Little did
I realize at the time just how important the sacrament of
Baptism is in our lives. Nor did I fully appreciate the wisdom of the Church in claiming newborn children for God,
following the tradition of our Jewish ancestors who were

explicitly instructed by God to consecrate their eight-day-old infants to him. This was an act that incorporated their babies into the Old Covenant, a covenant fulfilled and perfected through the life, death, and resurrection of Christ.

I returned to the Church while pregnant with our third daughter, Gaby, and shortly after her birth, Bernie asked a priest he was working with on a fundraising project to baptize our three girls, ages four months, two, and three. Bernie came home that evening and announced, "Father Tom is going to baptize the girls on August 27." That conversation constituted the entirety of our baptismal preparation. And while I didn't object, I had absolutely no understanding of the significance of Baptism or of the implications that it held for our children's lives.

As God would have it, our little daughters were baptized on the Feast of St. Monica, the endlessly praying mother of St. Augustine, a renegade son who would eventually become a bishop and Doctor of the Church. I always say that we don't pick the saints—they pick us! God clearly foresaw how much I would need St. Monica's intercession and how much she would have to teach me about the strength of a relentless mother's prayers.

Baptism . . . Saves You Now (1 Pt 3:21)

Like so many other Catholics, we "sacramentalized" our children with little or no catechesis, or teaching, about the meaning of the sacraments. I vividly remember the white linen dresses the older girls wore, the family baptismal gown we put on Gaby, and the party we had at my parents' house afterward. But I remember very little about the baptismal ceremony itself, except that my Aunt Verna said several times to me, "It's really good that you're having the children baptized," a sentiment over which I smiled and nodded but didn't comprehend.

I now understand exactly what Aunt Verna meant. Next to the days of our conception and birth, our baptismal birthday is probably the most important day of our lives. That's because at Baptism we are consecrated to God and born again: re-created in the image of Christ, made holy, and set apart for his purposes. Moreover, Baptism frees us from sin, makes us God's adopted children, and empowers us—through the Holy Spirit, who takes up residence in our souls—to act, live, and love as God's own family members. Baptism infuses in our souls the theological virtues of faith, hope, and charity, enabling us to participate in God's own self-understanding, to live with the firm conviction that heaven is our home, and to love God and others with the supernatural love of God. Further, Baptism incorporates us into Christ's Body and marks us with an indelible spiritual mark that can never be erased—a mark that forever seals us as God's property and possession. Baptism also capacitates us to share as priests, prophets, and kings in the mission of Jesus, equipping us to bring God's presence to the world and to its people in order to make them holy, as well as to announce the good news of salvation through Christ and to rule and reign with him, both now and in eternity.[4]

I offer this small overview of the powerful effects of Baptism to make an important point: God does not take our baptismal vows lightly, nor should we.[5] Baptism makes

us God's own sons and daughters, and just as we do not
let our children get lost or move into destruction without
parental intervention, God does not allow us to lose our
way without continually intervening and pursuing us,
ever calling us back to himself. This should give us great
hope in praying for our children. When life gets dark and
hope seems dim, we can and should call upon the power of
their baptismal vows as we pray for them, reminding God
to whom they belong and the promises that were made
either directly by them if they were old enough or by us
on their behalf if they were infants (not that God forgets,
but we often do). One of the prayers I habitually pray for
my children, especially when they are facing struggles, is
as follows:

> Lord Jesus, I call upon the power of [child's name]'s
> baptismal vows. I pray that the waters of [child's
> name]'s Baptism will rise up like a mighty river
> within him/her to bring faith, hope, and love alive
> in him/her and to protect him/her from temptation
> and all evil. Amen.

In the event that our children are not baptized, we should
consecrate them to God and pray that they be protected by
the blood of Jesus, shed on the Cross for their salvation. It
is also very effective to entrust them to Our Lady, placing
them into her Immaculate Heart, a safe refuge for sinners:

> Lord Jesus, I consecrate [child's name] to you and
> claim him/her for your kingdom. I cover [child's
> name] in your precious blood and ask that he/she
> be converted and come to living faith in you. Please
> protect him/her from all evil. I also place [child's

name] into the Immaculate Heart of Mary, asking
that Our Lady guard [child's name] under her mantle of peace and protection. Amen.

Train a [Child] in the Way He Should Go…He Will Not Swerve from It (Prv 22:6)

Many parents fret about their children as they grow older,
especially if they abandon the faith in which they were
raised or lose their faith in God completely. Our culture
seems to practically promote the forsaking of Christian
faith and values, as many of those in society have an
unspoken, or sometimes overt, agenda of deconstructing
the Christian faith in the next generations. Sometimes it
feels as if we are swimming upstream against a culture
that threatens to sweep the faith away entirely. How do
we hold on to faith? What's a parent to do?

Pray, pray, pray, for one thing, and never give up.
"The fervent prayer of a righteous person is very powerful," St. James tells us, just before he says, "If anyone
among you should stray from the truth and someone bring
him back, he should know that whoever brings back a sin-
ner from the error of his way will save his soul from death
and will cover a multitude of sins" (5:16, 19–20).

I think of St. Monica, whose son, Augustine, left his
home in Hippo at the impressionable age of seventeen to
study rhetoric in Carthage, a city that he referred to in his
famous *Confessions* as "a cauldron of illicit loves." Within
a short time, and much to his devout Catholic mother's
consternation, Augustine took a mistress, had a child out
of wedlock, and adopted the heretical gnostic religion of

Manichaeism, which, among other things, claimed that all matter is evil (contradicting the Christian belief in the Incarnation, which holds that God assumed human flesh).

St. Monica prayed and wept for seventeen long years for Augustine's conversion and was famously told by her bishop, "It is not possible that the son of so many tears should perish." Though Augustine tried to buck and escape his mother's Christian influence, Monica chased him by boat to Rome and then to Milan, where he eventually converted, was baptized, and consecrated himself exclusively to God. He would become one of the greatest saints in the history of the Church; and his mother, a patron saint of mothers. We know the details of St. Monica's life through the conversion story written by Augustine himself, an account of the potency of a mother's prayer to call forth life-changing grace that is still as pertinent today as it was fifteen hundred years ago when it was written.

Do you have an Augustine in your life? Have you been an Augustine yourself? I had a few of my own "Augustine years," so take heart: God pursues us relentlessly to break through our darkness, as St. Augustine so eloquently wrote:

> You called, shouted, broke through my deafness;
> you flared, blazed, banished my blindness;
> you lavished your fragrance, I gasped; and now I
> pant for you;
> I tasted you, and now I hunger and thirst;
> you touched me, and I burned for your peace.[6]

Here We Have No Lasting City (Heb 13:14)

Many parents ask what to do about their children who are less than enthusiastic about their faith or have ceased to practice it at all. Besides persistent prayer, surrendering them to God, and setting a vibrant example of Christian faith ourselves, I tell them to be patient, for time and life's difficulties will bring ample opportunities for our children to turn to the Lord. In fact, it is frequently when our children become parents themselves that they find the way back to their faith again. There is no better time for people to clarify what they believe than when they have to teach it to someone else or when they realize they are responsible for forming another soul as they face the mission and responsibility of parenting. I have seen this dynamic play out many times, including in the life of our youngest daughter, Gaby. While Gaby never ceased practicing the Catholic faith, becoming a mother brought her faith to life in a whole new way.

Gaby was only nineteen when she returned home from her first year of college with the news she was pregnant. While a baby is always a gift and a blessing, I grieved over the difficulties I imagined she would face as a single mother and worried about what the future would hold for her and for her baby. Providentially, I happened to be studying in a PhD program in Rome at that time, which required me to travel to the Eternal City four times a year. On each visit to Rome, I made a pilgrimage by foot to pray at the tomb of St. Monica (on whose feast day Gaby was baptized), which is located in the Church of St. Augustine near the picturesque Piazza Navona.

The first time I entered the church, I was surprised to see a famous seventeenth-century painting by the artist Caravaggio hanging over the side altar. The work, titled *The Madonna of Loreto*, is also known as *The Madonna of the Pilgrims* due to the dirty, ragged pilgrims in the scene bowing in adoration before the infant Jesus and his Mother. Caravaggio caused a scandal when he painted the piece because his realism, especially in the grime he painted on the feet of the pilgrims, seemed to suggest that Mary and Jesus were too close to us in our human mess. And that was precisely his point. The scandal of the life and death of the God-man is that Christ identifies completely with broken humanity, meeting us right in the middle of our muddle. He is with us in our sin and devastation and, in fact, has taken it upon himself.

Kneeling before *The Madonna of the Pilgrims*, I entrusted Gaby and her baby to Our Lady. I then moved on to the tomb of St. Monica to beg her intercession for them too. I could never have imagined that the day Gaby would go into labor, her dad would suffer a massive heart attack, changing our lives forever. Nor did I foresee at the time just how much Gaby would need to lean on her faith in God as she traveled her own pilgrim path through life.

Gaby's son, James, was born on Christmas Eve, while Bernie lay in extremely critical condition in the same hospital one floor below. She then spent the first three months of James's life caring for him at home without my help—not at all what we had planned. Thankfully, my sister, JoJo, and James's father, Grayson, were on hand to assist her in caring for the baby throughout Bernie's illness and death, amid extraordinarily challenging and stressful circumstances, to say the least. All I could do was surrender Gaby, Grayson, and James constantly to God's care, praying that he would somehow help them work out the details of their lives. And he certainly did.

Gaby and Grayson married six months after Bernie died and have since welcomed three more beautiful children to their family, two sons on the Feast of the Assumption and the Feast of the Ascension respectively, plus a baby girl this past Holy Saturday. Though they moved out of state after their second son, John-Henry, was born, we visit frequently, and I marvel at their faith each time we're together. It is especially gratifying to witness them passing on their beautiful, lively faith to their children. In fact, I've never been so surprised in all my life as the day James, John-Henry, and Joseph, who were five, two, and one at the time, sang the ancient chant "Christos Anesti" in perfect Greek during our family vacation—which they had learned on an iPhone while riding in the van with my son-in-law, Grayson. The big boys chanted in unison, while little Joseph danced, singing a hymn that is translated as follows: "Christ is risen from the dead, / trampling down death by death, / and to those in the tombs, granting life."

Oh, how we would need that reminder one short year later, when much to our shock and dismay, Grayson discovered he had a testicular tumor; this occurred one week after he and Gaby learned they were pregnant with their fourth child—news that knocked us all to our knees in prayer with its inherent challenge to trust God more deeply. The morning after Grayson's surgery to remove the tumor, I woke up in their home beset with grief and fear, as I anticipated the yet-unknown outcome of his biopsy, which the doctor had already warned us would probably be positive for cancer. Thankfully, their parish church has eucharistic adoration every Tuesday, and I was able to steal away for an hour to drag my heavy heart to the Lord.

"What in the heck is going on, Lord?" I started in angrily. "You *know* how much trauma our family has been through!" I continued with frustration. "Enough is enough! Didn't you get the memo that our period of suffering is over?" I complained to God for most of the hour while he listened patiently. Then he politely reminded me of the meaning of faith.

"Faith is a participation in God's own self-understanding." I heard the words I've spoken in lectures many times coming right back at me. "Trust that *I am love* and that I will only work this situation for good," God gently nudged. In that very moment, I turned to God and begged for trust, asking him for the faith to see the entire situation through his perspective, instead of through the lens of my own fear of suffering. Immediately, peace came—not by magic but by grace; and not through some world-endorsed formula for success or happiness but by way of heartfelt surrender to a Father who is infinite love and who loves me and all my family members immeasurably more than I do.

Faith—the supernatural ability to understand God as he really is, as love—is the very gift we give the generations when we consecrate them to God in Baptism. This great gift must be cultivated through teaching, practice, and example as we pray—and trust—that their faith will come alive as they face the trials of life that beckon them to personally experience God's tender love and goodness. Praying for living faith means that we ask God for more than our children's belief in him; we must also ask that they completely surrender to him and to his purposes, purposes that are sometimes revealed only when our programs, plans, and agendas are painfully stripped away.

Nothing Is Far from God (St. Monica)

Our worst fears were confirmed when Grayson's biopsy revealed that his tumor was, indeed, cancerous. His first appointment with the oncologist to determine a treatment plan was, God-incidentally, on the Feast of St. Monica, who famously said, "Nothing is far from God"—not cancer, not any dreaded diagnosis, and not even death itself. Nothing is far from God. That message bears repeating over and over again.

Thanks be to God, after two surgeries and a long, painful recovery, Grayson is cancer free. His unexpected illness reminded us again that life can be a messy, arduous journey, that the gift of life is fragile and precious, and that we must constantly beg God for the eyes to see our lives through the lens of his promise that he will work all things together for our good (Rom 8:28)—a promise that can be incredibly difficult to believe in the midst of great suffering and that is impossible to believe without faith.

While it is very human to ask "Why, God?" when life lunges forward in ways we didn't anticipate or that we interpret as disastrous, the grace of trust is possible in these moments if we open our hands and hearts, let go, and surrender to God. I have watched such trust form in my daughter and her husband as they have faced numerous difficulties; and I have simultaneously watched God, in his faithfulness, meet every single one of their needs.

As I write these words, Gaby and Grayson are on a three-month, cross-country excursion that will take their family from coast to coast, ending in Philadelphia for Pope Francis's Meeting with Families in America a year to the day after Grayson's second surgery.

Being far from civilization, having few creature comforts, living together in a twenty-six-by-eight-foot camper, being unable to run to the grocery store when they want (or need) something, and not having the luxury of taking a nice, hot bath every day are some of the minor discomforts they have faced. They also had no access to electricity or running water at certain campsites for days at a time— with four young children for which to feed and care! But God continues to provide for them and lead them on the path he's set for their life, with all that the journey entails.

And You Yourself a Sword Will Pierce (Lk 2:35)

Our Lady's entire life with Jesus was a pilgrimage—a state of "being on the way" under God's guidance that kept her ever traveling toward the fulfillment of his will. From the moment the angel Gabriel announced Jesus' miraculous conception in her womb to the day she surrendered the all-holy fruit of her womb on the Cross, the Blessed Mother's task was to abandon herself in trust to the superabundant provision of *Jehovah-jireh*, the name God revealed to Abraham after he obediently placed his son, Isaac, on the altar, which means, "The lord will provide."[7]

As I reflect on Mary's life, I wonder what she thought at the Presentation as she pondered Simeon's words that her soul too would be pierced—a prophecy that carried with it the double implication that her soul and the soul of her beloved Son would both be pierced. Was she tempted to worry about the meaning of those words throughout Jesus' life, to worry about the future, as so many of us mothers are prone to do? Surely, if most of us had a dollar for every second we spend worrying about our children, we'd be millionaires! But the secret to peace—a secret I'm confident Our Lady knew—is to live in the present moment, to be fully present to the present, for it is only in "now" that God resides.[8] Also, we must remember that when we consecrate our children to God, they become his very own children, children that he guards as the apple of his eye and whose names are carved on the palms of his hands.

While we may spend endless hours worrying about the future, the future is a phantom, a figment of our imagination that often robs us of our present peace. The choice to trust God is before us in each moment of each day, as we rely on his grace and promise to "fully supply whatever [we] need, in accord with his glorious riches in Christ Jesus" (Phil 4:19). This is exactly the way Our Lady teaches us to live.

Making Space for Love

PONDER

Will I entrust God with my children and their lives today, even when the future is uncertain and my heart is pierced with sorrow? Will I trust him to take care of my family, knowing he has promised to protect us and to provide for all that we need? Will I let God lead our lives with his loving providence, believing he is good?

PRAY

Father in heaven, thank you for the power of prayer and for your faithfulness to answer the cries of a mother's heart. I ask you now to protect my children from the evil influences of this world and especially to keep them safe under Mary's mantle of love. I call upon the power of their baptismal promises, asking that their baptismal graces flow like a river through their souls, bringing new life. Wash away any darkness or deception, Lord, and fill them with your light. I entrust my children to you, Lord, and ask you to hold them in your hands and heart. Especially when they walk through the dark valley, Lord, increase my trust, and theirs, that you are right beside them. Lead them in the path of truth and open their ears that they may hear you calling them by name. Increase in all of us faith and hope, Lord, that we may surrender to you entirely and live as though heaven is our home. And fill us with your divine love through the power of the Holy Spirit, who has been given to us that we may love you above all else and love our neighbor as ourselves. May we keep our eyes on you as we make our way toward heaven on this pilgrim path of earthly life. In Jesus' name I pray. Amen.

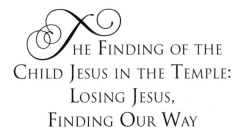

THE FINDING OF THE CHILD JESUS IN THE TEMPLE: LOSING JESUS, FINDING OUR WAY

Son, why have you done this to us?

~Luke 2:48

The doorbell rang, and I spied an unknown man at the front door. We had just returned from a long day at the hospital, where Bernie's son, Marshall, lay dying. Exhausted and despairing over Marshall's prognosis of probable brain death five days after he lapsed into a coma from liver failure, I was lamely attempting to prepare dinner. I couldn't imagine what this stranger could possibly be doing at our home.

"Are you Christian Klein's mother?" the man asked as I opened the door.

"Yes, why?" I responded tentatively.

"I'm Detective Black from the police department," he continued as he showed me his badge. "Is your husband home?" he asked. "I'd like to speak to both of Christian's parents."

After inviting him in to sit down, I went to our bedroom to retrieve Bernie, who was attempting to get some rest. As we sat in the living room, a new nightmare unfolded.

"The police department is investigating a number of petty crimes in your neighborhood, including the removal of beer from a garage refrigerator on Choctaw Lane and the disappearance of a bicycle from a garage on Longwood," he began. "We have reason to believe that your son was involved in these incidents."

As he spoke, our son Christian, who was a month shy of fourteen, entered the front door.

"Sit down, Christian," Bernie instructed. "There is an officer from the police department here with some questions. I want you to answer his questions truthfully."

Christian sat down sheepishly, and the detective read off a litany of incidents that had recently occurred in our area, all of which pointed to Christian and a few of his friends—and all of which Christian swore he knew nothing about. Seeing he was getting nowhere with his questioning, the officer finally stood up. "Here's my card, son," Detective Black said as he handed Christian a card with his phone number on it. "If you remember being involved in any of these incidents, you can call me anytime, day or night," he offered before exiting the house.

Upon the detective's departure, Bernie and I grilled Christian for the better part of a half hour, trying to impress upon him the importance of telling the truth if he had participated in any of the offenses. He'd been involved in some mischief lately, and we suspected he wasn't being completely honest, but we assured him that his consequences would be lessened if he told the truth. He held to his story, and eventually our family ate dinner and went to bed.

Around midnight, as I lay in bed praying the Rosary—anxiously begging for Our Lady's intervention for Marshall and for Christian—Christian barreled through our bedroom door. "Mom!" he practically shouted. "I was in the kitchen getting something to eat, and when I turned around, a bright light flashed in front of me! I heard a voice in my mind telling me to call that officer and tell him the truth. I need to call the detective immediately and tell him I was involved in those crimes," he continued excitedly.

On that note, we called Detective Black back to our home. By two a.m., he had booked Christian with a list of charges and released him back into our custody. Five days later, we buried Marshall.

Your Father and I Have Been Looking for You with Great Anxiety (Lk 2:48)

Imagine Mary's anxiety and sadness when life went terribly wrong. Imagine traveling in a caravan with relatives and friends for an entire day thinking your twelve-year-old son was among the crowd, only to discover that he was missing. Surely, most of us have experienced losing a child in a shopping mall for a few minutes and the ensuing panic inherent in trying to locate the child who has vanished. But three days of searching? Really? Joseph and

Mary must have been terrified. And where did they finally find their Son? Back in Jerusalem in the Temple, questioning the Jewish teachers and astonishing everyone with his insight and wisdom. You can almost hear Mary saying, "Son, why have you done this to us? Your father and I have been looking for you with great anxiety" (Lk 2:48). This wasn't the first sword to pierce Our Lady's heart. And it wouldn't be the last.

Jesus' separation from his parents at age twelve marks a point of growth in his life that we would refer to today as the beginning of "separation and individuation." In other words, it was a moment of deeper awakening to his own identity as the Son of the Father—an identity that would supersede his identity as Mary's Son. This moment in his life points forward to his mission as Savior of the world, in which he would undergo a future three-day disappearance into the tomb, an event to which Mary would also be called to surrender in the midst of extreme anxiety and grief.

Jesus was in his Father's house doing his Father's business when he went missing, but adolescents today are often caught in the foolishness of the world when they veer off course. Today's youths encounter a tenacious pull from the world that vies for their allegiance as they grow to maturity, a tug that can be treacherous and can threaten to pull them under in so many ways. Diligent, persistent prayer is needed by Christian mothers during what can prove to be difficult, dangerous adolescent years. God hears these prayers, and in his perfect timing, he answers.

Jesus Remained Behind in Jerusalem, but His Parents Did Not Know It (Lk 2:43)

I remember a neighbor once sharing at a party about his sons sneaking out of the house during the night, getting themselves in loads of trouble. My response? "How in the world could your children sneak out of the house without you knowing it?" I would learn that lesson myself a few years later—the hard way.

We discovered after the detective's visit that Christian had been climbing out of his bedroom window in the middle of the night and jumping off the second-story roof to meet his friends on the golf course behind our home. I remembered seeing a ladder against the back of the house one day and asking, "What in the world is the ladder doing out?" It never occurred to me that my young teenager was using it to climb back into the house!

Several weeks after Marshall's death and in the midst of emotional devastation, Bernie and I caught Christian in a few more sneaking out incidents, adding to his problems and the problems in our home, which had already been escalating for some time. We decided to send our son to live at a Catholic youth ranch in Wyoming for a year, figuring that an expansive cattle ranch in the West would provide a safe refuge to help divert him from the destructive path he was following.

The ranch, named after Our Lady of Mount Carmel, offered a wilderness program, a Catholic homeschooling education, and hands-on work as a ranch hand. It was run under the tutelage of a beautiful, holy couple named

Jerry and Mickey, who, while having seven children of their own, took in so many troubled young men over the years that they finally had to build a bunkhouse near their home to accommodate the growing crowd. The stunning landscape of the fifty-thousand-acre spread, which is not far from the entrance to Yellowstone National Park and is surrounded by a majestic view of the Grand Teton Mountains, made it seem like a perfect fit for our physically active, thrill-seeking son. Plus, the fact that a small monastery of Carmelite monks lived on the property—monks with whom our son would attend daily Mass—made it an extremely appealing draw for two desperate parents.

In spite of the obvious benefits of Mount Carmel, we delivered Christian there a week before his fourteenth birthday with much angst and sorrow, feeling we had failed completely as parents. Leaving our young teenager across the country proved to be much more excruciating than Bernie or I expected, and we both sobbed openly during the entirety of the four-hour plane ride home. The poor flight attendants kept asking if there was anything they could do for us, but nothing could ease our pain. The only thing that gave me any consolation during the trip was a scripture verse that echoed continuously in my mind: "I have lifted up my eyes to the mountains, from whence help shall come to me" (Ps 121:1).

We returned home to grieve Marshall's death and what felt like the loss of another son as well. It was then that I really began to get a slight glimmer of what Our Lady must have felt when she buried her beloved Son, and I began to understand in a way I'd never known before what it really means to release a child into God's hands.

Christian would live in the wilderness for seven months in rustic, primitive conditions before graduating to the bunkhouse to live for another seven. We visited him four times during those fourteen months, and it never got any easier to say good-bye.

His Mother Kept All These Things in Her Heart (Lk 2:51)

I knew very little about Our Lady of Mount Carmel before our son went to the ranch, but one of the first things I did when we came home was to conduct some research about the devotion to her. I learned that Mount Carmel, which is in the Holy Land, was the site of the first Carmelite hermits—a group of laymen who gathered on the mountain in the twelfth century to live in prayer and contemplation in honor of both Our Lady and the Old Testament prophet Elijah.

Mount Carmel is the site of the famous confrontation between Elijah and the wicked queen Jezebel, who seduced Israel into worshipping the pagan god Baal through practices that included deviant sexual rituals, human sacrifice, and self-mutilation—all meant to control the fertility gods. In the biblical account in 1 Kings 18, Elijah and the prophets of Baal engage in a dramatic showdown between good and evil, each calling upon their gods to consume the sacrifice they had placed upon the altar of worship. Only the God of Israel shows up, sending fire down from heaven to consume the sacrifice, proving his reality and his power and prompting the people to fall prostrate on their faces to proclaim, "The LORD is God! The LORD is God!" (verse 39).

As I read about what happened on the mountain of Carmel, it resonated with me that in our day and age, we are also confronted with a dramatic choice: God or idolatry, life or death. Our teenagers, who are particularly vulnerable to the pull of the prevailing culture, can go either way—and plenty of them go the *wrong* way, especially when they come face to face with the gods of power, pleasure, possessions, and perversion that have reared their heads in increasing ways during the past century; these false gods beckon for attention and allegiance.

Aware he was facing a critical choice, I prayed constantly that Christian would choose God, that he would choose life, and that his life would bear witness to the power and goodness of God. I placed him under the mantle of Our Lady of Mount Carmel, and though I had consecrated my family and myself to Mary's Immaculate Heart over a decade earlier, it seemed that God was calling us now in a special way to place ourselves under her banner as Queen of Carmel.

In my research, I also learned that Our Lady of Mount Carmel is associated with the brown scapular, which it is believed Mary gave to St. Simon Stock during a vision he had of her in the thirteenth century. Mary promised that everyone who wears the scapular receives particular protection from her, especially at the moment of death, because wearing it indicates a special sign of devotion and consecration to her.[9] Pondering all this, I remembered my deep interior struggle to embrace Mary upon returning to the Catholic Church. I also vividly recalled how much my life and heart changed when I finally "got it."

Behold, from Now On Will All Ages Call Me Blessed (Lk 1:48)

While it was the Blessed Mother who brought me back to the Catholic Church, I still kept her at bay for some time after my return. I had two major problems with the whole "Mary thing"—one in my head and one in my heart. The head problem was that there were still strong echoes of Protestantism in me, and I was both afraid of "Mary worship" and unable to understand how it was possible to have a relationship with Mary (or any of the saints for that matter) without offending Jesus. The heart problem was that there still lay in me the residue of rebellious feminism that I had learned growing up in the sixties and seventies; this feminism purported to liberate women sexually and set them free from the shackles of male domination and motherhood, and this feminism simmered with a seething if silent resentment toward men, connecting equality with men with becoming one of them.

When I reflected on Mary, she seemed so different from the women I had known in life, as well as from me. Truth be told, I didn't really want to be like Mary, as I feared that embracing her meant becoming a doormat or a wallflower, with neither seeming the least bit attractive given my strong, assertive personality and my proud history of feminist family members. Furthermore, was it really okay to love Mary, to consider her my Mother and imitate her? While I had no problem thinking of St. Paul as my "father" in Christ Jesus, considering myself one of his "beloved children," and trying to imitate him (as he directly admonishes the Christian community to do in 1

Corinthians 4:14–16), I was more than a little hesitant to do that with Mary, given the strong warnings I had received about her in Protestantism.

The head problem was the easier one to resolve. By studying scripture and reading numerous books by Protestant converts who had made their way into the Catholic Church, I came to understand that Jesus instructed the beloved disciple John to take Mary as his Mother just before he died (Jn 19:27), giving her not only to St. John but also to all disciples. I began to wonder why Protestants don't call Mary the Blessed Mother, since the Bible explicitly quotes her as saying, "from now on will all ages call me blessed" (Lk 1:48). I learned that Catholics are forbidden by the Church to worship Mary or anyone else but God but that we pay Mary the highest honor among God's creatures *because* she is the Mother of Our Savior—which seemed proper and reasonable to me. I also discovered that asking Mary or any other saint in heaven to pray for me was no different than asking another Christian on earth to pray for me—except that those in heaven, who are perfectly united to Christ, have far more powerful prayers than those on earth, who are still hampered by sin.[10]

If "the fervent prayer of a righteous person is very powerful" (Jas 5:16), then whose prayers could possibly be more powerful than "the spirits of the just made perfect" (Heb 12:23)—those who are perfectly righteous because they are in heaven? I was amazed to discover what the Bible says about exactly whom we approach when we come before the throne of God in prayer. While I had previously thought of my relationship with God and my prayer life as an "only Jesus and me" proposition, that is not the way scripture portrays it. What the Bible says is that when we approach God in the "heavenly Jerusalem," we approach "countless angels in festal gathering, *and* the assembly of the firstborn enrolled in heaven, *and* God the judge of all, *and* the spirits of the just made perfect, *and* Jesus, the mediator of a new covenant" (Heb 12:22–24, italics added).

Clearly, my either/or paradigm concerning Jesus and Mary was wrong, because when we pray to God, we stand before the Holy Trinity *and* all the saints and angels gathered in heaven, including Mary. So why shouldn't those in heaven, whom scripture refers to as "so great a cloud of witnesses" (Heb 12:1), be able to pray for us? The way the Bible portrays it, the saints in heaven can see us as we strive to "persevere in running the race that lies before us" (Heb 12:1). Why wouldn't they be praying for us and cheering us on as we run? Those in heaven, called the Church Triumphant, are still part of the Body of Christ, and the Body continues to function together as one organism, with Christ as the head. I began to see that the Catholic Church's teaching on Mary and the Communion of Saints was not only biblical but also made logical sense!

After much study, it became obvious that Jesus and Mary are not in competition for our loyalty and that to love Mary does not constitute idolatry but instead honors the Lord to whom she gave birth. On simply a human level, how many of us get offended because someone loves our mother, for crying out loud? Jesus is delighted when we love Mary, and Mary, in turn, desires only for us to love and serve her Son, because he is God. They both know that if we follow Mary's instructions and "do whatever he tells

[us]" (Jn 2:5), we will see the supernatural, transforming power of God at work in us and in the world around us, just as the wedding stewards who were present at Jesus' first miracle did. No wonder Satan hates Mary and wants "to sweep her away with the current" (Rv 12:15). Drawing near to her maternal heart brings us closer to the miraculous realm of Christ, which the enemy wants to prevent at all costs.

Finally, I began to ask, is God really so puny and small minded that he hoards his glory, keeping it all to himself? My conclusion was, of course not! He takes delight in showing forth his glory through his creatures, in magnifying himself through the souls of those who love him. Hence, Mary's proclamation in her Magnificat that her "soul magnifies the Lord" (Lk 1:46) suggests there is something akin to a magnifying glass on Mary's soul, through which we can see God's brilliance and glory more clearly. That should be true of all Christians, as it gives more honor and glory to God.

All of this began to make sense to me, and it seemed not only reasonable but also right.

Mary, the Woman for All Women

The second nut to crack—the heart problem I had concerning Mary—was harder, as it involved serious questions about my identity as a woman and about my own ongoing conversion. Would I be willing to be changed that I might embrace Mary as the model of my own femininity? Was I prepared to lay down the notions of womanhood in which I had been formed, making space for something new, such as accepting the idea that Mary's way—and not the way of radical feminism—is the life-giving way for women? And would I let Mary lead me by the hand as I sought to love Jesus and as I tried to help my children find Christ in a post-Christian culture that has lost him almost completely? It was in the midst of pondering these questions not long after my return to the Catholic Church that someone mentioned to me St. Louis Marie de Montfort's "Total Consecration to Jesus through Mary."

Anyone who has made the thirty-three-day consecration to Mary's Immaculate Heart can tell you how powerful and life changing it is, just as the women in our parish Rosary group told me one providential day. Peggy, who had recently made the consecration herself, was sharing with the group what a profound impact it had on her relationship with the Lord and how much personal healing she had received by making it. Always looking for ways to grow deeper in faith, I went to the Catholic bookstore and bought a copy of St. Louis Marie de Montfort's little gem of a book *Preparation for Total Consecration*.

While I must admit that I was somewhat taken aback by de Montfort's seventeenth-century language of making oneself a "slave" of Mary, as well as by the thought of giving myself entirely to her, I was prompted by the Holy Spirit to complete the consecration. Jesus tells us to judge a tree by its fruit (Mt 7:18), and shortly after consecrating myself to Mary amazing fruit began to appear in my life.

The first thing I experienced was long-sought-after forgiveness for the men who had hurt me in life, especially the person who had abused me. Though I had prayed for several years to forgive in obedience to Jesus' words, "If you forgive others their transgressions, your heavenly

Father will forgive you" (Mt 6:14), I still felt nothing but
intense anger toward the perpetrator. And while I know
that forgiveness is an act of the will—not a feeling—I
desired to be free of angry, negative emotions and their
impact on my life and family. I clearly remember the day
the feelings came that matched the decision I had made to
forgive, and they in no uncertain terms came on the heels
of my consecration to Mary.

I was alone in our master bedroom when I was
spontaneously overcome with such a powerful sense of
mercy and forgiveness for my abuser that it caused me
to drop to my knees weeping in prayer. It was as though
a river of pent-up hurt was released from my heart all at
once, matched by a river of tears. Not long after that day,
I started to become aware of the unfavorable, combative
thoughts I entertained about men as they were occurring
in my mind. I began to renounce them as they took shape
interiorly, extracting myself spiritually and emotionally
from the "man-hating" feminism that had formed me. I can
emphatically say that all this lent itself to what happened
next—letting go of my defenses against the authority of
the Church, including and especially the men who run it.
This ushered in what I like to call my "third conversion,"
that is, accepting the teaching of the Catholic faith in its
entirety, including its magisterium or teaching office. (My
first adult conversion was when I gave my life to Christ
in an evangelical church at the age of twenty-three. The
second was when I returned to the Catholic Church five
years later.)

In the long run, accepting the Church's authority led
me to experience liberating healing in so many areas of

life, especially in my relationship with God the Father. My consecration to Our Lady caused the dominoes to begin to fall in my heart and mind, softening me and making me more pliable in the hands of God. And isn't this the very essence of Marian spirituality? We, like Mary, utter an unceasing "may it be done to me" to the Lord, letting God have his way in us?

I can't say that it happened all at once, but the change in me was nothing short of miraculous. And instead of costing me my voice, my power, and my independence, as I had feared, giving myself to Mary caused me to become more completely yoked to Christ, who gave me an authentic voice, true power, and real freedom.

So why do we need Mary? We need Mary because her love and example humanizes us, tenderizes us, and makes us more welcoming of Christ. She teaches us in flesh and blood what it means to be a Christ-bearer—one who receives the Word, believes the Word, conceives the Word, and gives birth to him in a broken, sinful world. Furthermore, she shows us how to persevere in suffering, and her intercession helps us to stand steady before it, especially before suffering that involves our children. For Mary, of all women, understands intimately how a mother is cut to the heart when she sees her offspring hurting.

Going to Mount Carmel proved to be a powerfully formative experience for our son, one that he still values very highly to this day. And while Christian would have a few more rocky years after he left the ranch, we would encounter the direct intervention of Our Lady of Mount Carmel again when he was nineteen, when she swooped in to save his life.

Consecrating my family and myself to Mary was both a life changer and a game changer for all of us, the fruit of which is still unfolding in our lives. After all, Our Lady's greatest joy is to point us to Jesus and say, "Do whatever he tells you."

Making Space for Love

PONDER

When in my life have I been most frightened that my children had lost their way? Have I consecrated my family and myself to the Immaculate Heart of Mary, or am I willing to consider doing so? Do I believe Our Lady's intercession can help save my family and me from danger and destruction? Have I seen Mary's intervention in our lives thus far, and what difference has it made?

PRAY

Lord Jesus, thank you for the gift of your holy Mother, whom you gave me as my very own Mother when you hung upon the Cross. Give me the grace to avail myself of her help during the trials and tribulations of my life. Jesus, while I know I can't love your Mother more than you do, I pray for a share in your fervent love for her. I place my children and myself into the refuge of her Immaculate Heart, asking that we be protected from evil and formed in her way of love. Lord, I give you the fears and wounds surrounding my femininity, asking you to heal any lies or distortions in me concerning my womanhood. Grant me the grace to embrace true femininity in the image of your beautiful Mother, that I may be a Christ-bearer like her. In a special way, I pray for a Marian spirit to be the defining mark of the women in my bloodline. Free us from all rebellion against proper authority and from any attitude that rejects life, and fill us with your life-giving love. I ask these things through the powerful intercession of Our Lady of Mount Carmel and in your holy name. Amen.

Chapter 6

HE CRUCIFIXION:
WHEN DEATH IS AT THE DOOR

Standing by the cross of Jesus [was] his mother.
~John 19:25

The phone rang and startled me awake from a dead sleep. It was three a.m. My hand was numb and indented from clutching the rosary, which had become my habit during the long nights since the deaths of my brother Stephen and his wife over two years earlier. These days I was always waiting—waiting for "the call."

"Mama," Christian said from the other end of the line. "I'm gonna die." I had no idea where he was or what kind of danger he was in, but I knew his situation was dire. He was mired in the darkness of addiction, and it was a crapshoot on any given day whether he would make it through the night.

"I'm gonna die," my son repeated. "I'm doing terrible things and I can't stop," he continued. I could hear the despair in his voice.

"Yes, Christian, you are going to die if you continue on the path you're on," I said sadly but firmly, certain it was true. "I pray that you choose life and not death, son, but you're the only one who can choose. I beg you to choose life. I'm praying for you, Christian. I love you."

With that, the call ended. I began to pray the Rosary, focusing on the crucifixion of our Lord, praying for the grace of perseverance for Christian, and for me. I tried to imagine what Our Lady must have been thinking and feeling as she witnessed Jesus' death, how frightened she must have been, and the agony she felt. Jesus had predicted his own death three times, saying he would "suffer greatly . . . and be killed" (Mt 16:21). She had heard that it was coming, but words were cheap compared to the reality of standing at the foot of the Cross.

A mother's greatest fear is the death of a child. Certainly, that has always been my greatest fear—a dread that has awakened me many nights in life with a tremble, paralyzing me with the thought that something terrible might happen to one of my children, especially the unimaginable: death.

Not only had I wrestled with this anxiety for many years, but also I had watched the reality unfold in the lives of three people in my most intimate circle: Bernie, my mother, and my dear friend Pat. I had witnessed the emotional devastation of dealing with a child's death up close and personally and watched the heartbreak that had ensued, permanently altering the lives of those it had affected. It was not something I ever wanted to experience firsthand.

Yet I wondered, was the circle closing in on me? I lay alone in the darkness, haunted by the question. Was it my turn to bury a child?

"How did you do it, Blessed Mother? Please help me!" I pleaded for grace, knowing I was completely helpless to save my firstborn son. Multiple rehabs and interventions had not worked. We had tried everything. Things had spiraled so far out of control after his dad died that I'd had to resort to tough love and put Christian out of our home. The hardest thing I've ever done, it was totally counterintuitive to a mother's natural drive to help save her child. But I genuinely believed that putting Christian out was his last hope for survival.

I'd hoped and prayed that the shock of being put on the street would scare some sense into the boy, force him to get help, and jolt him into sobriety. It didn't. He found others who were willing to take him in, found enablers who were more than willing to supply him with money and drugs.

The only weapon left was prayer.

I surrendered my son for the gazillionth time to Jesus and to Our Lady, asking them to help and protect him and to intervene miraculously in his life. I hoped against hopelessness that something would break through, change, and move. I wanted a miracle for Christian so much and prayed for it so hard that it hurt. My head, heart, and womb ached. "Jesus, I trust in you," I prayed. "Jesus, I trust in you." I repeated that mantra again and again through the long, sorrowful nights until I could fall asleep.

My God, My God, Why
Have You Forsaken Me? (Mk 15:34)

Sleep hadn't come easy since we lost Stephen and his wife, Brenda, to murder-suicide on March 15, 2007. The news of their tragic ending came three days earlier, just after I'd gotten into bed. I'd wondered why the phone rang at ten thirty p.m. and then concluded it was nothing important after my husband fielded the call quietly from the den. When I heard the sound of my sister's voice in our bedroom ten minutes later, I knew something was dreadfully wrong.

"What's wrong? Did Daddy die?" I asked as soon as she entered my room, wondering if my eighty-year-old father had passed away. Unimaginably, JoJo reported in a weak, shaky voice that my second-eldest brother, Stephen, had just shot and killed his wife. He had called our parents to tell them what he'd done, and they immediately called the police and proceeded to race over to his house, fearing he would kill himself too.

"What?" I bolted straight up in disbelief, disoriented by the news and trying to assimilate it. "How can that be possible? How can that be?" I sprang to my feet as if lightning had hit me and then hurled myself back across the mattress onto my stomach as Joanne repeated the news, not knowing whether to stand or collapse.

"No, no, no!" I screamed, feeling dizzy and disoriented. "Why in God's name would Stephen shoot Brenda?" I demanded to know. She had been the love of his life for twenty-five years, and he'd spent the past few years waiting on her hand and foot as she became more and more debilitated by chronic back pain and an ensuing addiction to painkillers. Their lives had been dedicated to each other, and none of us had ever heard them speak so much as an irritable word to one another.

"Judy, he told me a couple of months ago that he and Brenda have been depressed since losing everything to Hurricane Katrina," she whispered, looking as if she'd seen a ghost.

"Oh my God . . . God have mercy," I whispered as I shook from head to toe. "Let's pray a Rosary right now," I said. All I could think to do at that moment was to beg for God's intervention and Our Lady's intercession.

"I'll lead it," I offered somberly. "Why don't we pray the Sorrowful Mysteries?"

We gathered our voices and spirits to pray for Stephen and Brenda and, trembling with fear, anxiously awaited some news.

"I believe in God, the Father Almighty, Creator of heaven and earth, and in Jesus Christ, his only Son, our Lord," we began the creed in unison, praying our way through Jesus' agony in the Garden of Gethsemane, the scourging at the pillar, the crowning with thorns, the carrying of the Cross, and the crucifixion. We concluded with the Hail Holy Queen and the Prayer to St. Michael the Archangel, begging him to "defend us in battle and be our protection against the wickedness and snares of the devil." The darkness of the night sat heavily upon us as we finished praying the Rosary.

The phone finally rang. My younger brother, Kenny, was on the line. "It's all over," he said crying hysterically.

"They're both gone." I could hear my mother wailing in the background. The line disconnected.

The next morning our extended family gathered in shock and grief at my parents' New Orleans home, where there were simply no words. I suggested we pray a Rosary, just as we'd done eight years earlier when Scott died. Somehow, quite unbelievably, here we were again. Only this time, things were worse.

I've learned over the years that when no words or explanations can be found, the words and mysteries of the Rosary say everything. When the mind is too stunned to think straight, the Rosary brings calming sanity. When the heart is shattered in two, the Rosary carries to it sweet consolation. When we encounter the bitter valley of tears, the Rosary helps us lay our broken hearts into the mercy and mystery of the fruit of Mary's womb. In our deepest sorrow, the Mother of God meets us right there at Calvary. She tenderly cradles us in her arms and weeps with us when we so sorely need her help. We ask for her prayers also at the hour of death, when we will need her assistance most. The Rosary provides a sacred covering for every fractured moment.

After Stephen and Brenda died that spring, the year ticked on with most of us surviving in a haze. Summer brought the news that Bernie had lost all the funding for a project he'd been working on for several years—bringing our income to a screeching halt and throwing us into a considerable financial crisis. Fall brought a serious escalation in Christian's addiction issues, forcing the necessity of several major interventions aimed at getting him sober. That winter, we were trying to get a grandbaby delivered the day before Christmas Eve when Bernie was slammed by a life-altering wound to his heart, bringing his life to an end on March 15, 2008—a year to the day after we buried Stephen and Brenda.

Had hell opened to swallow us up in some cruel cosmic joke, I wondered? Was God trying to destroy us completely? I was in the midst of asking these serious questions of God when Our Lady's promise came into sharp focus: *I will cleanse your family*. Somehow, I'd imagined that such cleansing would mean that God would wave his benevolent hand over our family to heal and convert everyone and answer all my prayers, just like that. I began to get a glimmer that real cleansing is more like standing in all-consuming fire, allowing God to burn away so much soul-clouding dross.

"Judy," Bernie had said as I entered his ICU cubicle early on Christmas morning, two days after the heart attack, "I've been praying the Memorare all night long, and all I can see every time I close my eyes is the Immaculate Heart of Mary." Then he dropped the real bomb: "Baby, I can feel my organs shutting down, and I know I'm dying."

Bernie prayed the Memorare continuously for the three days while he was still conscious, begging Mary for her help. Though he was what you might call a cultural Catholic, practicing his faith sporadically and without much conviction, he had developed the habit of praying the Memorare several times daily after Marshall's death—a practice that increased over time as our problems escalated. And while my husband never seemed to break through to a personal awakening of an intimate love relationship with God for which I constantly prayed (which I attributed in large part to the difficult relationship he had with his acutely alcoholic father), he did have a devotion to Our Lady. That happy fact was owed mostly to his devoutly Catholic Colombian mother who prayed a Rosary for him every day of her life.

The Memorare had become his favorite prayer in recent years, and to my knowledge, it was the only prayer he prayed the last few years of his life:

> Remember, O most gracious Virgin Mary, that never was it known that anyone who fled to thy protection, implored thy help, or sought thine intercession was left unaided.
> Inspired by this confidence, I fly unto thee, O Virgin of virgins, my mother; to thee do I come, before thee I stand, sinful and sorrowful. O Mother of the Word Incarnate, despise not my petitions, but in thy mercy hear and answer me.
> Amen.

It was this simple prayer to Our Lady that brought heaven's help when Bernie needed it most desperately, bringing him to fully yield to God at long last.

In Thy Mercy Hear and Answer Me (Memorare)

Sadly, the doctors confirmed that Bernie's organs had indeed begun to shut down. Two days later, his heart, lungs, kidneys, and liver had failed, and the only hope left was a heart transplant, for which my barely alive husband was transferred to a heart specialty hospital in New Orleans. Though doctors there did everything they could to save him, including shocking his heart three times to keep it beating the first night he arrived, they concluded Bernie was too sick for a transplant and focused all their efforts instead on just keeping him from dying—no small task when four major organs have ceased to function and life is being sustained entirely by mechanical means (which for him included a ventilator, a heart pump, a dialysis machine, and numerous medicines to keep his blood pressure at a life-sustaining level). Bernie spent the next six weeks completely comatose, hanging onto life by a thread.

A month and a half later and against all odds, Bernie miraculously woke up from his coma and began to speak, stunning the medical staff by coming back from what a nurse had bluntly referred to as being "basically dead" when we arrived at the heart hospital. I would learn that our heavenly Mother had not left Bernie unaided but had instead led him to see the spiritual condition of his own heart before leading him to another heart—the Sacred Heart of her Son, Jesus, which he could see every time he closed his eyes after awakening from the coma.

Though still gravely ill, Bernie was neurologically sound and able to communicate clearly, which earned him the name "Miracle Man" among the medical staff who cared for him—the moniker that eventually became the title of a book I wrote about the experience. Within days, Bernie shared with me what he called a "near-death experience," wherein he watched his soul leave his body and was shown with great clarity his own divided heart, including the good and evil therein. Bernie followed a golden light all the way to heaven and was stunned to be told by God that he wasn't permitted to enter. He was instructed to go back and make amends for his life, whereupon he encountered terrifying darkness, as well as creatures that inhabit the underside of the eternal realm, as his soul returned to his body.

As Bernie conveyed the astounding experience to me in graphic detail, especially his horrific battle with the dark side, all I could say was, "How did you resolve it?"

"I surrendered to God," he shared honestly and humbly. "And when I did I had so much peace. Judy," the miraculously resurrected man continued calmly, "this is my purification. And I *need* it." With that, the Blessed Mother's words to me over two decades earlier rang right in my ears: *I will cleanse your family.*

Then and there I began to comprehend that cleansing comes as stripping, depleting our arsenal of survival resources so we more readily turn to God for help. Often, it is then and only then that we will open our hands to God, discovering the mystery and miracle of surrender within the yielding act. Suffering thus becomes a vehicle for abandoning ourselves in trust to God, and the grace-filled means through which we learn to depend on him. It is in these precious moments of permitted purification—and there is no other way—that we discover God's radical faithfulness to his promise to use suffering for our good. We find the resurrection of our souls through the crucible of the Cross—which we come to experience in purest truth as the door to life and love.

My prayers were tenderly answered in a way I could have never expected but in the particular way that Bernie and I each needed for our healing and sanctification to take place. And in the face of such outrageous grace, the remnants of my own deep wound of mistrust in God finally

found a cure, as scales fell from my eyes and I began to
proclaim with utmost faith the words of Job's conclusion:

> I know that you can do all things,
>   and that no purpose of yours can be hindered.
> I have dealt with great things that I do not
>   understand;
>   things too wonderful for me, which I cannot
>   know.
> I had heard of you by word of mouth,
>   but now my eye has seen you.
>
> ~Job 42:2–5

Did I Not Tell You That If You Believe You Will See the Glory of God? (Jn 11:40)

Two days after Christian's nocturnal phone call, my dear
friend Mary Lou called. A recovering alcoholic I'd known
in college, she had providentially come back into my life
a month before Bernie's heart attack. Christian's addiction
was hitting a boiling point at the time, and I cried out to
God to send me a friend who had journeyed through the
disease of addiction. That very night I received an email
from Mary Lou, to whom I hadn't spoken in years, telling
me that our sons had met in a rehab hospital in Mississippi. She shared that she was also in recovery and offered
to help me in any way she could. I called her immediately, and she became my constant companion as I walked
through the dark valley.

That particular week, Mary Lou was asking me to
accompany her to a First Friday Eucharistic Adoration and
Confession service in New Orleans. A gifted priest and
exorcist named Father Joe, whose healing services we had

begun to attend regularly, would be leading it. I jumped at the chance to go, hoping that perhaps the sage priest would have some words of wisdom for me.

On Friday evening, we entered the rectory chapel of the old Blessed Francis Xavier Seelos Church that sits on the edge of the French Quarter. The church is named after a German priest who died in the city in the nineteenth century while caring for victims of yellow fever and whose cause for canonization awaits another miracle—maybe ours? I prayed silently on my knees before the Blessed Sacrament before getting into the queue for confession. When my turn came, I entered the dark room where Father Joe sat quietly waiting, hidden in the shadows of a dim lamp, and immediately broke down.

"Father, I've buried my husband, two brothers, and my stepson in the past few years," I hunched over and sobbed to the Irish-born priest, who already knew my story in detail due to my visits with him to have Masses said after Stephen and Brenda died. "I can't bury my son! I just can't!" I cried, unable to restrain my emotion.

"Stop!" Father Joe said kindly but forcefully in his soft Irish brogue as he raised his palm in the air toward me for effect. "Give the boy to me and let me take him to the Lord. You go home and grieve the death of your husband!"

"Okay," I said haltingly through my tears as I sat up straighter, somewhat surprised at his reaction. Rethinking it for a second, I replied with more conviction. "Okay . . . I can do that." And I gave the boy to Christ's priest, standing in his person.

As soon as I did I felt a dramatic shift, as though a heavy weight had been lifted right off of me. The burden of carrying Christian instantly disappeared, and I drove the forty-five minutes to our home feeling peaceful, confident that Christian and I would somehow both be okay. I slept through the night without worrying, certain that Christian was in God's hands—hands big and merciful enough to carry him securely.

A Sign of Contradiction

Though I didn't completely understand it at the time, I had received the breakthrough for which I had been praying. God had answered my prayer for a shift, all right, and the shift had occurred in *me*. Something changed when Father Joe told me to give my son to him, and in my desperation, I agreed. Right on the spot, instantaneously, I experienced the miracle of sweet surrender in releasing Christian into God's hands, scattering the panic that had gripped my soul in recent months, seeking to steal back trust. Somehow that blessed yes had at last crucified my notion of how things had to be, bringing forth the fruit of freedom in the recognition of my powerlessness.

Miraculously, when I released Christian from my grasp I began to trust viscerally that no matter what happened to him, he would be okay. A deep sense of assurance came over me that I need not be afraid, for this situation, just like every painful situation I'd ever encountered in life, was not too big for God. It was the same change I experienced days before Bernie's death when I stopped insisting that my will be done in demanding that Bernie be healed and definitively gave him over to God. The change that yes brought about in me was so noticeable that our nurse, Holly, even commented, "You were nowhere near ready to say good-bye to Mr. Bernie when you first got to this hospital," she said. "But I can see that you are ready now." Just like that, I had finally let go. And when I did, I experienced the movement of amazing grace as the miracle that moves mountains, found in the blessed fiat—the yes that changes things.

Had I discovered the secret to Our Lady's assenting posture as she stood at the foot of the Cross? Had I received a glimmer of her graced consent and the endurance it ushers in? One of the root meanings of the word *endurance* is "to harden"—and it is such holy hardening that suffering brings forth. Not a hardening of the heart or a muscling up against God in the face of deep affliction but a spiritual strengthening that carries with it inner fortitude and proven character, the precursors of hope (Rom 5:3–5).

Within days, Christian called again, and it was crystal clear to me that he heard the transformation in my voice. Instead of agony, my voice and heart bespoke confident hope and trust in God, indicating that I had stepped out of the matrix of his addiction into the atmosphere of surrendered reliance upon God. The conversation was short but different. It was as though the Velcro upon which the insanity of his addiction had found its place to crash into me for so many years had been torn off, leaving no place for it to land.

Two days later, Christian called again.

"Hi, Mom!" he said excitedly. "Guess who I just hung up with?" he asked.

"I have no idea," I replied. "Who?"

"Albino, who runs Comunita Cenacolo," he continued. "I called him and scheduled my orientation at the community for next week. Will you bring me to Florida on Sunday?"

"Of course I will!" I answered without hesitating, even though my chin was on the floor. I had called Albino two years earlier to put Christian's name on the waiting list but had been told that Christian had to *want* to enter the Catholic community for recovering addicts and that the community would not take him unless he entered willingly. I had prayed incessantly for that miracle too but couldn't even begin to imagine how it would come to pass.

"I'm not going to go to some Jesus camp, Mom! I can promise you that," Christian said unequivocally every time the subject came up. "That is *never* going to happen," he vowed.

Four days after Christian called Albino, Mary Lou and I were on the road with him, headed to Comunita Cenacolo in St. Augustine, Florida. We were to drop him off at a house named Our Lady of Hope first thing Monday morning—the same house that Mary Lou's son, John, had entered a year earlier. The house is one of sixty-five group homes that have sprung up around the world since a little Italian nun named Mother Elvira Petrozzi started the community over thirty years ago—founded, of all days, on the Feast of Our Lady of Mount Carmel.

Italian for "the Community of the Cenacle," the hallowed refuge came to exist through the yes of one small sister who, like Blessed Teresa of Calcutta, had received "a call within the call." Hearing the Lord speak to her while already a religious, she founded the community to reach out to the poorest of the poor in the Western world—the hopeless, the despairing, the addicted, the isolated, and the lonely. Opening the first house in an abandoned estate on a hillside in Saluzzo, Italy, Mother Elvira moved into the dilapidated old mansion with a handful of addicted young men to begin the laborious process of rebuilding the house, and their lives, from the ground up. Thirty plus years later, thousands of people have come through the community's doors, experiencing the healing power of faith, hope, and love as they journey from death to life through the discovery of authentic love of Christ, lived out through deep prayer, hard work, and vibrant community life.

The road trip there was treacherous, as we drove twelve hours through the pouring rain with anger and despair seeping out of every crevice of my poor son's soul. The initial sense of excitement for a new start in life quickly dissipated when the reality of detoxing from hard drugs began to set in, creating heavy tension and frustration that saturated the car. All I could do was take Mary Lou's advice and sit quietly alone in the backseat with my headphones in my ears, listening to a continuous stream of praise music while I let her drive and talk to Christian. He finally fell asleep as night began to fall, and Mary Lou and I could at last lift our voices together in prayer, asking for Our Lady's help as we drove headlong toward St. Augustine praying the Rosary repeatedly.

Would Our Lady of Mount Carmel show up to once again help my broken son? Would she have mercy upon us and lead Christian finally to his namesake, Jesus Christ? Would she place her foot squarely on the serpent's head that my beloved child be delivered from the clutches of death and find instead true life? We dropped Christian off at Our Lady of Hope at nine a.m. sharp on Monday,

June 7, to begin his three-day orientation in prayer, work, and community. Mary Lou and I then went off in search of Mass and a perpetual adoration chapel to prayerfully await what the Lord would do next.

Blessed Is the Womb That Carried You and the Breasts at Which You Nursed (Lk 11:27)

I discovered that the city of St. Augustine was founded by Spanish Catholic missionaries on the Blessed Mother's birthday, September 8, in 1565. The old city is also the home of the first shrine dedicated to Mary in the United States, the Shrine of Our Lady of La Leche, translated "Our Lady of the Milk" and named for Mary as a nursing mother. Mary Lou and I quickly found our way into the exquisite open-air memorial, which draws thousands of visitors each year, many coming specifically to pray for their children. What a perfect setting for us to spend three days waiting for Christian to complete his orientation, time that would be spent praying that he'd agree to make the three-year commitment necessary to enter the community.

We spent our days moving between the shrine and the adjacent Prince of Peace Church, which happily had perpetual adoration of the Blessed Sacrament as well as daily Mass. Mary Lou and I devoted our days to interceding for Christian and our families, including Mary Lou's five sons and especially her eldest, John, who was living at Our Lady of Hope at the time.

Monday went well, but by Tuesday evening Christian had grown agitated and distressed over the prospect of leaving his life to live in a cloistered community for the next three years. Our conversation grew conflictual as the evening wore on, and by dinner's end, Christian abruptly stormed out of the hotel to get into a waiting vehicle— God alone knows whose—to disappear into the darkness. Fearing what might become of him, we proceeded to pray a Rosary and beg God for his protection. He made it back during the night, but I braced myself for the possibility that he would refuse to return to the community for his last day of orientation.

Mary Lou and I got up early the next morning to attend Mass before Christian woke up. I'll never forget the first reading that morning, as it was the showdown between Elijah and the prophets of Baal on Mount Carmel that had come to mean so much to me when Christian lived in Wyoming. In the scene, the prophet Elijah prays,

> LORD, God . . . let it be known this day that you are God. . . . Answer me, LORD! Answer me, that this people may know that you, LORD, are God and that you have brought them back to their senses.
>
> ~1 Kings 18:36–37

Here I was again, taking Christian to a refuge instituted under the banner of Our Lady of Mount Carmel, feeling the battle rage for his life and begging God for an answer. I entrusted him once again to Our Lady's care and returned to the hotel.

Much to our surprise, Christian was dressed and ready to return for his final day of orientation when we arrived, and we dropped him off as planned. We were told to come back for lunch, at which time Christian would let us know his decision about entering the community. If he agreed to enter, he would be sent home with me to get his personal affairs in order and return on an agreed-upon date, usually two weeks in the future.

We came back for lunch as instructed, and then Christian and I joined Albino and Brendan, the young man responsible for running the house, in Albino's office to hear my son's decision. Albino and Brendan had a short conversation in Italian and then turned to confront Christian.

"In my twenty years at Cenacolo, we've never let someone enter the community at orientation," Albino began. "But you're not going to make it back here alive in two weeks if we let you go home, Christian," he continued. "We're asking you to make a decision to enter the community today. You'll be dead before you get back here otherwise."

Christian looked at me totally surprised, taken aback by what just happened. "Do you think I really need this, Mama?" he asked innocently, looking like a little boy.

"Yes, Christian, I think you need this," I said gently. "As Albino said, you'll die if you don't get help."

"Okay," Christian said, stalling for time. "I have to make one phone call and smoke a cigarette before I decide." With that, we walked outside the perimeter of the gate, and half expecting him to run, I sat beside my son on a felled tree next to the highway. "I don't know if I can stay three years, Mom," Christian started in. "That's a long time."

"Please, just try it, Christian," I pleaded. "You might be surprised at how fast it goes."

Christian made one phone call to say good-bye to his best friend, telling him that he loved him and that he'd be gone for "a long, long time." And with a final puff of his cigarette, he walked into the welcoming arms of Our Lady of Hope—at three o'clock sharp. Mary Lou and I drove off the property praying the Chaplet of Divine Mercy.

It was finished. It was time for my son—and me—to begin our new lives.

Making Space for Love

PONDER

Have I been able to turn to God more deeply during moments of personal crucifixion in life? How have I experienced his presence, or his miraculous intervention, during these times? Have I discovered the power of the Rosary to change and transform my heart? How has Our Lady's love helped me during times of intense crisis?

PRAY

Lord Jesus, you alone know the depths of crucifixion because you alone died on the Cross bearing the weight of the sins of the world. I bring to you now the crosses I am carrying, especially those I am experiencing as crushing and overwhelming. I give you my most heart-wrenching trials and tribulations, placing them upon your Cross so that you might take these burdens from me. Lord, bring healing and redemption into the broken areas of my life as I choose to exchange the weight of my worries for your yoke, which is easy. Lord, you promise rest for my soul if I give my burdens to you, for your burden is light. I surrender my burdens to you now and ask you to give my soul sweet repose from travail and worry. Move mountains in my life, Lord, and work miracles that I don't even know how to ask for. Give me the grace of complete trust in you and belief in your mighty power, which alone can save me and those I love. In a special way, I surrender my children to you through Our Lady of Sorrows, placing them in her arms at the foot of the Cross that she might present them to you. Help me to discover the power of your Mother's intercession, especially through her most powerful Rosary. I love you, Jesus, and I thank you for dying on the Cross on behalf of my children and me. I release all into your sacred hands, and I beg for the grace of the power of your redemption to heal and transform our lives. In your holy name I pray. Amen.

Chapter 7

THE RESURRECTION: HOW GOD MAKES THINGS NEW

Now in the place where [Jesus] had been crucified there was a garden.

~John 19:41

Silence. That is what we hear from God's Word about the Blessed Mother following the death of her Son. We do not see her at the empty tomb, and there is no biblical account of Jesus appearing to her at the Resurrection. There is, however, a longstanding tradition in the Church that Jesus appeared first to his Mother after he rose from the dead. Such a belief has been affirmed by a number of great saints, including St. Anselm, St. Albert the Great, St. Ignatius Loyola, St. Teresa of Avila, and St. John Paul II. In fact, in 1571 St. Teresa of Avila had a mystical experience of our Lord's passion that made her acutely aware of the loneliness and desolation experienced by Our Lady at the foot of the Cross. On this same occasion, the Lord told her, "On my resurrection I went to our Lady who was in great need . . . and I stayed long with her for she was in very great need of consolation."[11]

While the Church cannot definitively confirm that which is not contained in revelation, it is permissible to believe what has been revealed privately to several saints, including St. Teresa of Avila, who is a Doctor of the Church. To my mind, it seems reasonable and right that Jesus would have appeared first to his own Mother, who not only cooperated perfectly in God's plan to redeem the world but also carried the Redeemer himself in the hallowed temple of her body. It also seems fitting that there is silence around Our Lady upon her Son's death and resurrection, for as the contemplative monk Thomas Merton so eloquently stated about Mary, "Her sanctity is the silence in which alone Christ can be heard, and the voice of God becomes an experience to us through her contemplation."[12]

What was Mary doing in the days after Christ's death? She was grieving, to be sure, as she pondered in her heart what had taken place before her very eyes, and as she, a human mother, took into herself the reality of the brutal, violent death her Son had suffered on the Cross. For here stood the woman prophesied about in the garden, about whom the Lord God had said,

> I will put enmity between you and the woman,
>   and between your offspring and hers;
> He will strike at your head,
>   while you strike at his heel.
>
> ~Genesis 3:15

Here Mary stood in a new garden, to place her offspring, Jesus, into the virgin tomb within. Her grief was real, and yes, there were no words. Sometimes it is only in silence that our hearts can tell the tale of the sorrows they hold. And too, in silent waiting, is the hope of resurrection.

Stop Holding On to Me (Jn 20:17)

I had no idea what to expect after I dropped Christian off at Cenacolo. I didn't know if he would stay or flee through the unlocked gates, which are always open in the event that someone wants to depart. It was early June, and I planned to see him at the family retreat in late October. Until then, there would be no communication between us, and I would simply have to trust Jesus and Our Lady to hold him.

I went home to grieve Bernie's death, as Father Joe had instructed. Home, such as it now was, housed only ten-year-old Benjamin and me. Silence was the new language of our domain, as Kara, Alex, and Gaby had all moved on to various places to live their lives. Our previously busy, noisy household was now dauntingly quiet, and it was quite a challenge to embrace the "new normal" of being the single mother of a lone child. A lonely summer loomed large before me, so I decided to take Benjamin to visit Alex, who was living and working in Jackson Hole, Wyoming. Alex had found her way to the majestic Grand Teton Mountains to grieve and to heal, and their stunning silence provided a needed repose for her soul as she grappled with all that had occurred in our lives.

Alex, who is sturdy and strong like the mountains, had stayed by my side until Bernie took his dying breath. Though she was not a child who took center stage in our family and has often joked that she is the family's "lost child," she's had a heart for the pain of others ever since she was a little girl—so much so that we nicknamed her "the public defender" because she constantly came to the defense of anyone who experienced pain in our family. Today she is a licensed social worker helping others heal from trauma, a perfect vocation for a young woman whose soul exudes a blend of quiet compassion and steady, hidden strength—in truth, much like Our Lady.

When we arrived in Jackson Hole, I told Alex that I wanted to take a hike, having in mind a nice leisurely walk beside a clear running stream. She took me instead for a trek straight up a mountain trail, a trudge that was more than a bit challenging given that I'm not athletic, am scared of heights, and am unaccustomed to high altitudes. Though I panted for breath and bemoaned the difficulty of the climb most of the way up, Alex insisted that we push our way up the peaks anyway. Not being one to turn back lightly in the face of a challenge, she knew from experience that the reward of climbing the mountain—the breathtaking, invigorating vistas—could only be seen from on high.

"Come on, Mom, you can do it," she said repeatedly as I huffed for breath. "Drink plenty of water," she coached. Because as any experienced climber can tell you, the essential factor in making it up the mountain is saturating oneself with an ample supply of water. I reflected upon how important water is to both our natural and our spiritual lives—especially in times of drought. God had given me so much living water during times of sorrow and suffering, slaking my thirst continually as I immersed myself in Christ and asked him to drench me in his love. That love sustained me during the two hardest uphill climbs of my life—surrendering Bernie to eternal life and Christian to new life, both rising from the jaws of death.

Our mountain trek also reminded me that food is indispensable for the journey, as it is necessary for both life and strength. "Stop and eat a snack," Alex insisted after an arduous period of climbing when I was feeling weak and disoriented, convinced that I couldn't go on. I recalled the long, painful days in the ICU, when the only thing that kept me going was Holy Communion—the superabundant Bread of Life mercifully delivered daily to Bernie's hospital room by a minister of the Eucharist. I do not believe I would have survived the suffering we endured without that supernatural food, just as I know that I would have been unable to continue climbing upward on the mountain with Alex without natural sustenance.

With Alex by my side, I also learned that if you're going to climb a mountain, it's best not to do it alone. If you get injured or lost, a companion can be utterly invaluable in both seeking and finding help. In fact, in the event that you simply can't go any farther, you may even need someone to carry you across the finish line. I thought about Alex's promise of personal presence in the days just before Bernie's death and how grateful I was for her tender love and support. "Don't worry, Mom," she said. "I'll be here with you and Dad until the end." Then she bravely sat beside us, offering her company as a gift in our vast vulnerability while we opened our hands to death—admitting unreservedly our powerlessness and mortality and giving rise to the opportunity for a child of our loins and hearts to *surrender* us to God.

They say "what goes around comes around," and I know that this is true. Offering becomes a two-way street in the face of human frailty, and it was Alex's turn to offer a parent back to God. At the foot of the Cross in a hospital room she cried, "God, behold my father." And from that very hour the Lord took Bernie into his heavenly home.

What Does It Mean to Rise from the Dead?

So what does resurrection look like, and how does it play out? I've come to understand that it is more of a slow rising from the ashes than a one-shot wonder and that it takes time for its reality to sink in. One must stand in the tension between the grief of death and the hope of new life to embrace resurrection's paradox: it is through death that we find life, by dying that we rise, and only by losing our life that we find it.

We ask for the gift of faith when we pray the Rosary's first Glorious Mystery—because it is faith that permits us to view reality through God's very own eyes. Faith widens the lens of our limited human understanding, giving us the graced view of eternal perspective to see that all is well in God. It's the unveiled revelation of living faith that allows us to see Christ in the midst of our pain, as our hearts open up to anchor themselves in the promise of life beyond the grave, which is the ground of hope.

Though Jesus thundered from the grave in an instant and the joy of the Resurrection was immediately known to some, he stayed with his disciples for forty instructive days because it took time for Easter's reality to penetrate their minds and hearts and for them to assimilate its meaning. It is enlightening to read the Resurrection narratives

in tandem to glean the disciples' reaction to his rising—
which they took in haltingly and fearfully, and only as their
eyes permitted them to see. Though our crisp white linen
clothing and Easter Sunday bonnets offer a rather starched
version of the Resurrection story, the event was definitely
no magic bullet for his followers, who could understand
only in glimmers what it meant to rise from the dead.
Doubtful, fearful, unbelieving, confused, amazed, rejoicing, bewildered, terrified, and astounded are the words
used to convey their reaction upon encountering the risen
Christ. And my favorite description of all, "incredulous for
joy" (Lk 24:41), seems to present an outright contradiction
in terms, given that incredulous means unwilling or unable
to believe.

There is an irony that the Resurrection accounts poi-
gnantly portray, and it is something we must confront.
Death is painful, confounding, and disorienting, even
when the story ends well.

I spent three years following Bernie's death prayerfully digesting what had happened during the splendidly
grace-filled finale of his earthly life. Also, I was mourning the stunning losses our family had faced, even those
that resulted in new life. I joined a widow's group, and
we spent Friday mornings lamenting our heart piercings,
praying Our Lady's Rosary of the Seven Sorrows. Over
time, the "weeping widows" began to gather for some
celebratory meals on Saturday nights, as large and small
victories began to appear in our personal lives.

"Was it not necessary that the Messiah should suffer
these things and enter into his glory?" the risen Lord asked
two still-befuddled disciples as he walked with them to

Emmaus (Lk 24:26). What they didn't yet comprehend is that, in Christ, suffering and glory are two sides of the same coin, as are dying and rising from the dead.

At Dusk Weeping Comes for the Night; but at Dawn There Is Rejoicing (Ps 30:6)

Christian miraculously stayed at Cenacolo, and he began to heal and thrive. He eventually moved to Italy, sleeping on a bed right beside Mary Lou's son John for an entire year and becoming "brothers" during their tenure together. My resurrecting son also began to lead the community's worship, becoming proficient on both the guitar and in singing as he learned to sing praise to God. The first time I witnessed Christian lead worship at one of the community's family retreats, I shed profuse tears of gratitude mixed with tears of awe, as I had never heard him sing a note before that day and had no idea he had such a beautiful voice. He found his voice thanks to the community, along with living faith in God. That is evident by the light now shining through the beautiful eyes that once heralded darkness, giving a glimpse into his soul.

And while it costs nothing to live in one of Cenacolo's houses, the community asks of us our own deeper conversion to Christ, indeed, the pearl of greatest price. Thus, in an intentional effort to ramp up my prayer life to meet Christian in his daily prayer commitments (which included at least an hour of eucharistic adoration and three Rosaries each day), I decided in early 2011 to become a daily adorer of Jesus in the Blessed Sacrament. Kara had come home temporarily at the beginning of that year, and together we committed ourselves to a daily hour of adoration, usually at different times of the day.

Kara had begun to pray that God would send me a new husband, even though getting remarried was the furthest thing from my mind. I was still healing and trying to assimilate what had happened in our lives, which was enough to keep my attention. One day Kara asked me what I'd want in a husband if I were to get remarried, and I assured her that Jesus alone could meet my needs. She pressed me to tell her what qualifications I would want in a man, and so I proceeded to name off a list: "he would have to truly love God, go to daily Mass and daily adoration, and be well versed in theology and philosophy" (I was studying for a PhD in bioethics at the time and figured that a similar educational background would be nice). "Furthermore, he would need to love to read, walk, cook," I continued, "and love the beach, coffee, and good wine," I continued, putting everything on the table I could think of that a perfect mate would be like. "Oh, and he must never have been married and have no children," I added, thinking of my already complicated life.

"Well, that's ridiculous," Kara replied. "You're never going to find someone like that!"

"That's exactly my point!" I retorted. "I'm happy to be married to Jesus for the rest of my life. Besides, Kara, what other man could possibly handle the drama and trauma of my life?" And on we went with our lives, which included daily adoration.

One day Kara came home to report that she had seen a new man in the adoration chapel several times and that he'd been there every afternoon lately when she went in to pray. "He wrote me a note to say he was praying for my intentions and asked me to pray for his upcoming job interview."

"Oh, that's interesting," I said. "Is he cute?" I asked, thinking the chapel would be the perfect place for her to meet a husband.

"No, Mom!" she exclaimed. "He's too old for me, anyway," she added. "I just noticed he's spending hours a day in the chapel."

One afternoon I accompanied Kara to the chapel to pray, and we happened to exit at the same time as the "new man." Kara, who'd had a brief conversation with him one day outside the chapel, introduced him to me.

I learned that his name was Mark and that he'd recently returned home to Louisiana after serving as a missionary for thirty years, most of those spent in Europe. Never married, he had spent years helping indigent children get off the streets, including eighteen years in the Soviet Union rescuing orphans and abandoned street children after the fall of communism. He had degrees in theology and philosophy, plus a master's degree in theology. He'd moved to our little town of Mandeville to be near the adoration chapel, where he was spending hours a day in prayer discerning what God had for him next. Mark was drawn to Mandeville because it sits on the edge of Lake Pontchartrain—the next best thing to the beach! The three of us struck up a friendship, and I immediately enlisted his help with my dissertation.

Our friendship began by reading articles by Joseph Ratzinger (Pope emeritus Benedict XVI) and discussing them over coffee and walks on the lakefront (which only two theology nerds would think was an absolute blast). Kara suggested that we begin to invite Mark over for dinner once a week, and he happily offered to cook. Weekly dinners and discussions about both my dissertation and our lives continued from May through December, and we became the best of friends.

One January day, I was praying in the chapel when I clearly heard the Lord speak. "I want you to love this man," God said, to which I replied, "Seriously, Lord?" Because while I loved Mark as a dear friend, I was not romantically inclined toward him, and quite frankly, I couldn't envision things going in that direction.

"I want you to love this man," I heard the Lord say so insistently over the next two months that I finally started to offer a new reply: "I can't *make* myself fall in love with him, Lord. But if that is truly your will, then, fiat, let it be done to me."

The Lord was so persistent in his request that I love Mark, with whom I was still strictly friends, that I finally asked God to confirm if what I was hearing was indeed from him.

On March 19, 2012, the third anniversary of Bernie's burial on the Feast of St. Joseph, I went to a different adoration chapel than usual with the intention of going afterward to St. Joseph's Abbey to visit Bernie's grave. I was having what I had come to call "a weepy day" and just wanted a quiet day of prayer and retreat.

Upon entering the chapel, I recognized a woman named Becky whom I'd spoken to more than three years ago and hadn't laid eyes on since. I had been in the chapel crying shortly before Bernie got sick, and Becky stopped me outside to ask if I was okay. I told her I was worried about my daughter Gaby, who was pregnant and unmarried. I was anxious about how things would work out for her and concerned about her future. Becky said she could see me holding a beautiful baby in my arms and told me that God wanted me to know that everything was going to be fine. Seeing her now three years later, I wanted to tell her that she had been right—that Gaby and Grayson had gotten married and had just welcomed their second son. But because we were in the chapel and she was praying quietly, I decided not to bother her. "If you want me to speak to her, Lord, then have her come up to me," I prayed. I then proceeded to close my eyes, crying silently as I recalled the days surrounding Bernie's death.

The next thing I knew I felt a tap on my shoulder and looked up to see Becky standing at my right. "Did you tell the Lord you wanted to speak to me?" she whispered, as I nodded yes with a look of surprise on my face. "Can you come outside for a moment?" she continued, and then she headed for the door. Amazed at what just happened, I followed Becky outside the chapel, where we stood face to face.

"What did you want to say to me?" she asked. I proceeded to tell her she had been right, that Gaby's story had indeed had a happy ending and that her baby, James, had brought so much joy into our lives. "Then why are you crying?" she questioned, looking perplexed.

"Because the day she went into labor my husband, Bernie, had a massive heart attack. He died three months later, and today is the third anniversary of his burial," I explained, wiping away tears.

"Well, the Lord told me to tell you that the next time I see you in here, you will no longer be crying," Becky said with a twinkle in her eyes. "You are getting ready to find the most exquisite love, and the next time I see you, you'll be levitating with happiness!"

I smiled and thanked her, saying good-bye to return to the chapel to pray.

Five days later, Mark and I made plans to attend Mass together for the Feast of the Annunciation, where a young, charismatic priest whom I'd never met before was celebrating a healing Mass. When the Mass ended he invited us to come up for prayer, and I followed Mark up to the altar.

Father Kyle put his hands on me to pray and then, rearing his head back, looked at me with a puzzled expression on his face. "Lord," he said boldly, "my sister already *knows* what you've asked her to do!" And then he repeated back to me the very prayer I had been praying: "So let it be done to her in the earth of her heart as it's already been done according to your holy will in heaven. Amen!" With that, I'd received my answer, and I knew that God was calling me to give my life to Mark.

I made the decision right then and there to say yes unreservedly if and when Mark began to pursue me romantically. Things changed very quickly between the two of us after that night, and I can only say that my feelings immediately followed the act of my will.

Mark and I became engaged in June and were married on the Feast of the Archangels, September 29, 2012, with all my children and grandchildren present. On our first anniversary, we traveled to Rome for a belated honeymoon celebration, and we were thrilled beyond words to meet Pope Francis and have him bless our marriage.

I can say unequivocally three years later that Mark has been one of the greatest gifts I've ever received from God. God knew I would find a best friend, a soul mate, and a husband who loves me as Christ loves the Church, as well as a holy man who loves and blesses my children as though they are his own. As Kara so eloquently shared on EWTN's *Life on the Rock* not long after Mark and I were married, "The Lord has brought this incredible stepfather into our lives, a man who is really holy and righteous and beautiful, and has taught me a lot in the short time he's been my stepdad. Christ is so very, very much first in his life, and it just shines forth in everything he does. It shows in the way that he loves my mom."

God knew this would be the case. And still, he waited for my yes.

Living Resurrection

Christian spent four and a half years in Comunita Cenacolo, living in Florida, Alabama, Italy, Austria, and Bosnia before his walk there came to an end. His journey afforded our entire family the amazing opportunity to attend many family retreats in America, as well as offering Benjamin, Kara, and me the wonderful grace of being present twice at the Festival of Life in Italy, a remarkable celebration of life in Christ we will surely never forget.

In no uncertain terms, the community has helped to heal and transform our family with its unambiguous challenge to believe in God's power to change our hearts and lives. The community has also challenged us to embrace our wounds and brokenness as a blessing, coming to see our children's addictions as a gift—the gift that led us to the family of Cenacolo and closer to Christ and his Mother. Further, Cenacolo has taught us to trust God more deeply by commending our lives to his loving Providence, which meets our every need. And as Christian beautifully articulated in a letter he wrote to me in late 2011, it has imparted to us and to our children the secret to peace, that is, surrendering everything to God: "I now put these things into the hands of God, and I realize that this has been my biggest change—surrendering everything into his hands. In this special time of Advent, being that it is a time of special graces, I am especially praying for the strength *not* to be afraid."

I can hear the echo of Jesus' words: Do not be afraid! In the face of suffering and uncertainty, do not be afraid! When winds are fierce and waters rage, do not be afraid! When confronted with death and destruction, do not be afraid!

We find such holy boldness not by depending upon ourselves but by learning to trust Christ's promises and by letting him form himself in us. For the mystery of the Cross is not that it kills but that it brings new life—life that makes us victorious over earthly afflictions, including the lingering consequences of original sin, namely, sin, suffering, and death.

The secret to victory is found in the words Jesus spoke shortly before his arrest. "In the world you will have trouble," Jesus told his disciples, "but take courage, I have conquered the world" (Jn 16:33). But how, we ask, did Jesus conquer the world when the darkness seems so prevalent?

Jesus conquered the world by dying on the Cross and rising from the dead, removing the sting of death by making it the pathway to ecstatic, eternal communion with God instead of the dreaded curse it was. He overcame the world by taking sin and suffering upon himself, making suffering a source of holiness, transformation, and union with God instead of an enemy to be avoided at all costs. Christ conquered the world by turning the world's understanding of these harsh realities right on their head, teaching us that when the cross presents itself in our lives, an opportunity is also present to unite ourselves with him and thus grow in faith, trust, and intimacy with the living God.

How does this happen? How in the world can suffering ever become sweet? It happens when we *turn toward* the cross and embrace it and discover ourselves graced with strength we hadn't imagined possible that enables us to persevere through the trial. It happens when we *unite* our sufferings with the suffering of Christ and then find ourselves filled with a steadfast trust and confidence in God that defies human circumstances. In these hallowed instances, we experience God's faithfulness to answer our cries for help. It is thus that we discover his power being perfected in our weakness (2 Cor 12:9) and, as such, we rejoice.

It is the experiential awakening to God working wonders in our woes that teaches us these truths—truths I learned personally in the midst of a worst-case scenario in life, when God's strength filled my inmost being with such force that I experienced the grace of spiritual triumph. While the world would label the path of suffering our family traveled as merely "loss" and "defeat," the hidden, victorious power of Christ transforming us from "glory to glory" (2 Cor 3:18) was all too real, and it changed every one of us.

Nothing less than Christ's resurrection was at work in our midst, bringing forth the fruits of joy and hope in the face of suffering and death. This is the mystery St. Paul describes in his letter to the Romans, where he writes, "We even boast of our afflictions, knowing that affliction produces endurance, and endurance, proven character, and proven character, hope." Moreover, he assures us that "hope does not disappoint, because the love of God has been poured out into our hearts through the *holy Spirit* that has been given to us" (Rom 5:3–5, italics added).

The last place Mary is explicitly mentioned in scripture is in the upper room, where the Church awaits this promised Spirit, whom Mary already intimately knows. There she meets with the infant Church as they devote themselves to prayer (Acts 1:14); and it is there that the disciples will learn what full surrender to God really means: that they might, like Mary, become bold witnesses of Christ.

With Mary in the upper room, Jesus' final words to his disciples find their fulfillment—words that echo those spoken to his Mother at the annunciation by heaven's envoy. "You will receive power when the holy Spirit comes upon you" (Acts 1:8; see also Lk 1:35), they are assured. Indeed, power from on high will fall upon the disciples, that they might unhesitatingly carry Christ to the world.

Our Lady has brought us full circle: Christ and his Church are birthed. Only the Mother of God is present in both places as the icon of human surrender. An important question remains, and it is a question that we each must answer: Will we open our hearts to Mary's example and love that we might become Christ-bearers too?

The promises Mary extols in her magnificent song are not just far-off, distant words—they extend to us and to our children right now, right here, today. Let us say yes to God with all our hearts and ask for the grace to behold his favor, blessing, and mercy. For he remembers the promise he made to Abraham and his children—and to our Mother Mary and her children—for all generations.

Let Us Pray: The Magnificat

My soul proclaims the greatness of the Lord,
  my spirit rejoices in God my Savior
for he has looked with favor on his lowly servant.
  From this day all generations will call me blessed:
the Almighty has done great things for me,
  and holy is his Name.
He has mercy on those who fear him
  in every generation.
He has shown the strength of his arm,
  he has scattered the proud in their conceit.
He has cast down the mighty from their thrones,
  and has lifted up the lowly.
He has filled the hungry with good things,
  and the rich he has sent away empty.
He has come to the help of his servant Israel
  for he has remembered his promise of mercy,
the promise he made to our fathers,
  to Abraham and his children forever. Amen.

Making Space for Love

PONDER

Was I surprised at this rendering of resurrection, as a slow rising back to life? Does my own experience of rising from the ashes of my suffering fit this description? What ashes of mine may God want to infuse with new life and beauty through the power of his life-giving Spirit?

PRAY

Lord, God, you promise to comfort all who mourn; to place on those who mourn a crown instead of ashes; and to give us oil of gladness in place of mourning, a glorious mantle instead of a listless spirit (Is 61:2–3). Lord, I surrender to you now every sorrow and every death I have known, asking you to mingle your precious blood with my tears, that my wounds may become glorified and life giving. I unite my tears also with those Our Lady shed at the foot of the Cross, asking that she would make them fruitful through her powerful intercession both in my life and in the lives of all generations of my bloodline. I thank you for the Resurrection and for the power you have given me to overcome sin and death. I thank you for your Holy Spirit, Lord, whose power to redeem and transform the brokenness of my life can turn my sorrows into a beautiful offering for you and for others. Fill me with your Spirit, Lord, and bathe me in your love. Grant me and those I love resurrection victories and the healing of our hearts. May my life and all that it holds be a pleasing offering to you, and may my faith in you convey a convincing witness of your redeeming love to this broken world. I ask these things through the Immaculate Heart of Mary, your tender Mother and ours. Glory be to the Father, and to the Son, and to the Holy Spirit, as it was in the beginning, is now, and ever shall be, world without end. Amen.

Acknowledgments

A book doesn't come to life by itself—it is the consummation of many life-giving yeses all along the way. It is thus that I offer:

Heartfelt gratitude to Lisa Hendey for saying yes in bringing me on board as a *CatholicMom.com* writer, introducing me to your wonderful book editor, Heidi Hess Saxton, and agreeing to feature this humble work as a *CatholicMom.com* book. Lisa, you set the bar high in demonstrating what it means to be a generous woman of God! Thank you for your help and example!

Immense thanks to Heidi Hess Saxton for saying yes in giving me a chance to write for Ave Maria Press. Without your extensive assistance, encouragement, and advice, this book would not exist.

Grateful acknowledgment to Jonathan Weyer and the terrific team at Ave Maria Press for your invaluable guidance in birthing this book, as well as for your daily yes in bringing this and so many other labors of love to fruition.

Deep gratitude to the many wonderful women through whom God has graciously blessed my life over the years (you know who you are!). Special thanks to those I've mentioned by name in this book and in previous work, including my two sisters and lifelong friends, Renee and Joanne. Your yeses have enriched my life immeasurably, and your companionship has provided the love, laughter, and support that kept me going when life seemed formidable. I thank you from the bottom of my heart.

Profound appreciation to my children, Kara, Alexandra, Gabrielle, Christian, and Benjamin for teaching me to be a woman of prayer and for saying yes in giving me kind permission to tell your stories. I love you more than words or prayers could ever express, and I thank God continuously for the incredible gift of your lives and for the unparalleled blessing of being your mother.

Inexpressible thanks to my husband, Mark. Your yes has blessed me in countless beautiful and life-changing ways, and I could never offer adequate gratitude for your friendship and love. Thanks for your patience in being the sounding board for everything I think and write! Thank you especially for your example of holiness, which inspires me daily to be more like Christ.

All glory and praise to the Father, the Son, and the Holy Spirit—the loves of my life, the reason I exist, and my hope for a future full of joy.

NOTES

1. Stormie Omartian, *The Power of a Praying Parent* (Eugene, OR: Harvest House Publishers, 1995), 24.

2. Peter M. J. Stravinskas, ed., *Our Sunday Visitor's Catholic Encyclopedia* (Huntington, IN: Our Sunday Visitor, 1991), 691.

3. Horatio Spafford, "It Is Well With My Soul" (1873).

4. See the *Catechism of the Catholic Church*, paragraphs 1262–74, for a full explanation of the effects of Baptism.

5. Our baptismal vows include the following promises:

V. Do you reject Satan?

R. I do.

V. And all his works?

R. I do.

V. And all his empty promises?

R. I do.

V. Do you believe in God, the Father Almighty, creator of heaven and earth?

R. I do.

V. Do you believe in Jesus Christ, his only Son, our Lord, who was born of the Virgin Mary, was crucified, died, and was buried, rose from the dead, and is now seated at the right hand of the Father?

R. I do.

V. Do you believe in the Holy Spirit, the holy Catholic Church, the communion of saints, the forgiveness of sins, the resurrection of the body, and life everlasting?

R. I do.

V. God, the all-powerful Father of our Lord Jesus Christ, has given us a new birth by water and the Holy Spirit, and forgiven all our sins. May he also keep us faithful to our Lord Jesus Christ for ever and ever.

R. Amen.

6. St. Augustine, *Confessions*, trans. Henry Chadwick (New York: Oxford University Press, 2008), 201.

7. Ronald F. Youngblood, ed., *Nelson's New Illustrated Bible Dictionary* (Nashville: Thomas Nelson, 1995), 503.

8. Catholic philosophers and theologians teach that God resides in an eternal *now*, wherein the past and future are contained in a perfect now. While man is a temporal being and therefore lives in time, God is eternal, existing outside of time.

9. "The Scapular promise is based on the two elements of Mary's spiritual maternity and her mediation of grace, that is that she is the 'spiritual' mother of all mankind, as well as the 'channel' by which all grace comes to us, understood in the sense that she too is dependent on the sole mediation of Christ, her son." "St. Simon Stock and the Brown Scapular," Theotokos Books, accessed January 26, 2016, http://www.theotokos.org.uk/.

10. I highly recommend convert Tim Staples's excellent book on Mary, *Behold Your Mother: A Biblical and*

Historical Defense of the Marian Doctrines (El Cajon, CA: Catholic Answers Press, 2014).

11 . "St. Teresa of Jesus and the Virgin Mary," Discalced Carmelite Order, accessed February 29, 2016, http://www.ocd.pcn.net/mad_en1.htm.

12. Thomas Merton, *New Seeds of Contemplation* (New York: New Directions, 1961), 168.

Judy Landrieu Klein is a Catholic author, speaker, theologian, counselor, and founder of Memorare Ministries. She received a master's degree in theological studies from the University of Dallas in 2000 and conducted post-graduate doctoral studies in bioethics at the Regina Apostolorum Pontifical Athanaeum in Rome. Certified as a temperament counselor by the National Christian Counselors Association, Klein is pursuing her PhD in clinical Christian counseling. She served as an adjunct professor of theology at Our Lady of Holy Cross College in New Orleans for seven years.

Klein's books include *Mary's Way, Living Water, Sez Who,* and *Miracle Man.* She has written for Catholic Digest and blogs at *CatholicMom.com* and *Aleteia.* She served as cohost of Radio Maria's *Apologetics Live* program for more than four years. Additionally, she has appeared on EWTN's *Women of Grace* and Focus Worldwide Television's *Focus.* Klein has been the featured speaker at many faith-based events, including Magnificat Women's Breakfasts, Legatus dinners, and Theology on Tap meetings. The mother of five and grandmother of seven, Klein is married to Mark Gelis and lives in New Orleans.